Geoffrey Smith's World of Flowers
Part One

Geoffrey Smith's World of Flowers

Part One

Edited by Brian Davies

BRITISH BROADCASTING CORPORATION

Published to accompany the BBC television
series *Geoffrey Smith's World of Flowers*
First broadcast on BBC2 early in 1983

Produced by Brian Davies

The programmes were prepared in consultation
with the BBC Continuing Education Council

© Geoffrey Smith and the
British Broadcasting Corporation 1983

First published 1983

Published by the British Broadcasting Corporation,
35 Marylebone High Street, London W1M 4AA

Printed and bound in the Netherlands
by Royal Smeets Offset B.V. Weert

Photoset in 10/12 pt 'Monophoto' Plantin Light
by Jarrold & Sons, Ltd, Norwich.

ISBN 0 563 16483 2

Contents

Introduction

Above: Geoffrey Smith in
a bulbfield in Holland

Title page: Finding *Cypripedium
calceolus*, the 'Lady Slipper' orchid,
in the Swiss Alps

Half Title: *Tulipa* 'Love Song',
a new *kaufmanniana* hybrid

All the colour photographs
were specially taken for the BBC
by Mel Davies, with the
exception of those provided by
Pat Brindley on pages 22, 23 (top)
and 58, and Ian Butterfield
on page 85 (top left)

Precisely when I first became conscious that the plants growing
in my garden had a history is difficult to remember. Certainly,
when a friend of my father brought back a selection of wild flower
seeds from Australia that awareness grew into a compulsive
interest – a desire to know more about the plants as individuals.
Where did they come from? What soil and climate did they grow
in? How did they come by names like 'Poor Man's Bean' and
'Kangaroo Paw'? The fact that names such as Forrest, Farrer,
Kingdon-Ward, Hooker, Ludlow, and others kept recurring at
regular intervals in connection with so many of my favourite
plants added another avenue to explore. For these were the plant
hunters, vital links in the chain of plant history, whose exploits
read like an adventure story.

Writing this book, and making the BBC television series
Geoffrey Smith's World of Flowers has been a dual experience. I
have visited places familiar from long association to search out
plants with which I have shared years of gardening familiarity.
Alpines native to this country are not very common, and
searching out the 'Spring Gentian' above High Force in
Teesdale took me over pathways I walked as a schoolboy. 'Bird's
Eye Primrose' growing in profusion between limestone outcrops
in upper Wharfedale made a picture which will long live in my
memory. Spring had touched the dale with a beauty all the more
captivating because high up on the fells it arrives shy and
hesitant, unsure of a welcome.

The dual experience came because not all the ground covered
was familiar. There were new places both at home and abroad, in
search not just of the growing plants – essential though they were
– but also the need to uncover the history behind them. This
revealed much information that combined fact, legend and
folklore. In some cases the three are so intertwined that it is
difficult to distinguish truth from fiction.

I am indebted to Bettina Wilkes and Elizabeth Farrar who
had the unenviable task of checking the manuscript. Also to
Frank Holland who worked so hard on the design, layout of
photographs and text of the book. Finally, my grateful thanks to
all the people who allowed us access to their gardens to photograph the flowers.

I
Alpines

An alpine, so far as the gardener is concerned, includes any plant capable of being cultivated in a rock garden, scree bed, or alpine house without looking incongruous. In botanical terms, the definition is more exact. Alpines are those plants which grow in extremes of climate where the growing season is curtailed – as, for example, in Arctic tundra, or above the tree line in mountainous regions of the world. The altitude at which plant life survives varies from sea level on the Arctic fringe to many thousands of feet above sea level in the Alps or Himalayas. With such a wide geographical range the variations in soil and habitat are enormous. A soil-packed crevice on a south-facing cliff in the Dolomites is vastly different from the conditions of soil and weather which exist in the peat bogs of the tundra. A plant growing in an exposed rock face must be capable of enduring months of sub-zero temperatures with no protecting cover of snow. In summer, hot sunlight reflecting from the bare rock has a dehydrating effect which would desiccate any but the most specialised plant. Screes and moraines, the great jumbled masses of stone which tumble down the mountain sides, are also colonised by plants. The stone slides are formed by the weathering of the bare rock. Extremes of heat and cold with constant attack from wind and rain slowly break down the solid rock. The broken fragments roll down the steep slope, eventually finding their angle of rest and stability. The stones composing the moraine or scree are of various sizes, from boulders weighing many tons to fine sand mixed with plant remains and forming a very quick drainage system for roots. This is compensated for in some degree by the mineral-rich moisture which percolates down through them from the melting snow above. Like the plants growing on the exposed rock face, those of scree or moraine have widely spread root systems which tap the underground water to support only a small amount of top growth. This is a feature of many high alpine plants: widely ramifying roots and small leaves providing only the minimum area to the dehydrating effects of sun and wind.

Moderately level plateaux where a depth of humus-rich soil has accumulated support a plant community that is less specialised but equally interesting from the gardener's point of view.

A meadow in the Swiss Alps

Indeed, this is the fascination of alpines – charming the eye with their beauty while challenging skill in cultivation.

Naturally, mountains composed of Dolomitic limestone are inhabited by a different plant community from that found on mountains which offer a neutral or acid soil. Fortunately, even in a small area the alpine enthusiast can provide the different soil conditions which suit a saxifraga from the Dolomites or a gentian from the Himalayas, all in the space of a few feet.

Considering the extremes of climate, exposure, and the immense variation in soil composition and chemistry, the type of plant life collectively described as 'alpines' is not surprising. What never fails to astonish me is how readily so many alpines will adapt to conditions in lowland gardens. That they do so while still retaining the charm, beauty of flower or foliage and compactness of growth which attracts gardeners in the first place is our good fortune. There are exceptions which, on being transferred to the lusher, less vigorous environment of the garden, do lose character. They grow coarse, fail to flower, and in general behave like a noxious weed. Others are incapable of making the change, trapped by the defensive mechanisms which enable them to survive alpine conditions. The felted or hairy foliage, a barrier to cold or sun at high elevations, traps moisture at lower altitudes.

Alpine plants are accustomed to clearly defined seasons with winter an unbroken dormant period. In the garden warm sunshine following frost persuades a plant winter is over, then a further burst of cold weather catches it in full growth. To counteract the worst effects which a change of climate and soil produces, the gardener should make the best provision possible. A porous, well-drained soil is essential, supplied with moisture throughout the growing season, yet not liable to waterlogging in winter. Although alpines do not as a rule need shelter from frost, some, however, do need protection from the constant dampness of lowland winters.

A well-constructed alpine house will give adequate protection to any plants which are seriously harmed by being too wet for long periods during the winter. An alpine house needs to be purpose built. Ventilators along the full length on both sides of the ridge, and side ventilation with additional louvre-style vents in the wall below staging level are, if not essential, extremely valuable. Mass-produced, general-purpose greenhouses are capable of being converted into an alpine house by the installation of a fan or air circulator as an aid to the existing ventilation system. Just to see the mountain plants which in a greenhouse flower in January, petals unspoilt by the weather, is complete justification for any indulgence necessary to ensure their good health.

Over the last thirty years I have constructed rock gardens using limestone, millstone grit, sandstone and tufa. They ranged in size from well over an acre to a modest little outcrop 6 feet by 8 feet (1·8 m by 2·4 m) in the middle of a lawn. Each time I have taken great care to ensure that the stones were laid in such a way as to reproduce the appearance of a natural rock formation. Certainly, after years of building, then maintaining rock gardens, the only advantage to accrue from all the labour was that the plants were presented in a 'natural' setting. Few things look more unnatural than a limestone outcrop in a suburban garden surrounded by carefully squared and trimmed hedges. Good-quality stone is extremely expensive and heavy to handle.

Bearing in mind the main essentials for the successful cultivation of alpines, good drainage, free air circulation, and full light can all be supplied by table beds which are raised a little above the general level of the garden, then filled with compost specially prepared to suit a plant's requirements. The bed, which can be constructed to any shape required in brick or stone, once established is pleasantly easy to weed and top dress. Hollow walls with a brick, stone, or breeze-block outer skin and the centre

filled with soil offer just the conditions which even some of the more demanding alpines find congenial. Of all the suggestions made for the cultivation of alpines, possibly a scree bed works best in practice. Construction is simple although a little laborious. On a sloping site simply dig out the soil to a depth of 20 to 24 inches (51 to 61 cm). Keep the top soil separate and dispose of the sub-soil elsewhere in the garden. I spread several dozen barrow-loads thinly over the vegetable garden, then mix it in while winter digging. The next step is to lay a 10- to 12-inch (25- to 30-cm) layer of broken stone in the excavation to provide drainage. On top of this is spread a layer of half-rotted leaves, coarse peat, or reversed turf – anything which prevents the fine compost from the top layer washing down into the drainage holes between the stones. The final stage is to mix the excavated top soil with stone chips, very sharp sand, plus a little peat as a moisture holder.

Aim at producing a very gritty, free-draining top 12 inches (30 cm) to the scree. This is a general-purpose mixture to suit the less demanding alpines. Pockets can be made with peat for those plants requiring more moisture; conversely, extra grit can be added as required for those plants which thrive in poorer conditions. Whether the choice of the construction falls on the traditional rock garden, scree, table bed, hollow wall, or just raking sand on to a sloping site in the garden, it will need supplementary care once the plants are established: weeding, watering in dry weather, then feeding and top dressing with freshly mixed compost to maintain the rooting medium in good condition. To anyone who thinks this is a lot of work and trouble just to grow alpines, I would say they are the most fascinating, diverse, yet at the same time exasperating of all the plants I have ever grown. From *Gentiana verna*, which grows in Teesdale, to the *celmisia* from New Zealand, they possess a charm which I find irresistible.

The specialist who desires to know more and more about less and less will find satisfaction in studying a single genus containing a large number of species. Campanula or saxifraga are examples of these. At the risk of suffering severe horticultural

Above and left: *Gentiana verna* growing wild in the French Alps

Right: *Pulsatilla alpina apiifolia*

indigestion I grow any of the mountain flowers available that attract me, and have not yet done more than discover what a wealth of beautiful plants there are.

The European mountains, which support several hundred species of garden worth, are sufficiently accessible for the enthusiast actually to go and see the plants growing naturally. There in an alpine meadow with snow-capped mountains beyond may be seen *Pulsatilla alpina*, *Saxifraga oppositifolia* and *Gentiana verna* forming a dark red and blue fringe to the clear water of an alpine lake. Alternatively, at the end of the day after a surfeit of flowers, one can wade through meadows of *Lilium martagon*. These are moments to recapture annually as the same plants grow to flower in your own garden.

For those who garden a soil which is naturally alkaline, before deciding whether to build a rock garden, table bed, or scree, it is my experience that only in a table bed is it easy to provide and maintain the acid, lime-free soil which is necessary to grow certain calcifuge (lime-hating) plants. With a suitable home prepared and ready, the most pleasant task of all is choosing those plants which will form a basis of our alpine collection. *Do not* under any circumstances go and dig up wild plants. All other considerations apart, in most countries now this is illegal. Look at the plants, then buy those selected from one of the many nurseries that specialise in alpines.

Many, even the choicest, can be grown from seed – the method I prefer. The shortest route to an intimate under-standing of a plant's needs is to tend it from seed packet to maturity. One special lesson that all would-be growers of mountain plants should learn is that rarity is no guarantee of beauty. Familiar, easy-to-grow plants which flourish in gardens all over the country would not be so popular if they were not good value. An example of this universal popularity is *Alyssum saxatile* from Eastern Europe, where it inhabits rocks and similar stony places. The leaves are grey-green and the flowers, which open during April and May, are a deep golden yellow. As would be expected with a plant which has been grown in British gardens for close on three hundred years, there are many named clonal forms: 'Citrinum' with yellow flowers; 'Dudley Neville' with buff orange flowers; and 'Plenum' which, as the name implies, is full double. Commonly seen in spring bedding, alyssum looks handsome as an edge to a rock garden, table bed, or hollow wall.

Of equal merit and widely cultivated is aubrieta, which grows in the wild from Iran to Sicily. The most important species in gardening terms is *A. deltoidea*, parent of so many garden forms. Few plants flower with greater freedom in spring, given a place in lime soil and full sun. They should be trimmed hard back after flowering to keep top growth neat. Named varieties or good coloured forms are best increased by cuttings or division. They make good carpeting plants, and look superb growing in a wall or rock crevice in association with alyssum.

Androsace enjoys a fairly wide distribution throughout Europe and Asia. I am familiar with several of these species, but have never succeeded with any from very high altitudes. Some

Lilium martagon

Androsace vandellii

are easy to grow if provided with a scree-type soil, others, from high up rock faces in the mountains, will not thrive outdoors in this country, and are better accommodated in a frame or alpine house. Undoubtedly, those I have grown are amongst the most attractive mountain flowers to have graced my garden. I first saw *Androsace alpina* growing 13 000 feet (4 000 m) up a scree on the Pointe des Lessières in the Val d'Isère in the French Alps. It has soft, hairy leaves covered in bright pink flowers. Only in its natural habitat does this gem so reward: in the garden it is what can best be described as a reluctant participant. Of equal charm, *A. vandellii* is more compliant, at least if grown in a gritty mixture in an alpine house. The dense cushion of grey felted leaves and myriads of white flowers, each with a yellow eye, is breath-takingly beautiful. The plants I found were growing in a vertical crevice across the face of a cliff 300 feet (91 m) high in the Alps. I grew stock from seed which flowered for three springs in the alpine house; I just never dare risk growing them in the open garden. This is part of the fascination which alpines have for me; even within a single genus there are species so difficult to grow that sometimes the specialists are driven to despair. As if to compensate, there are others so delightfully easy to accommodate that they flatter our gardening ego. *A. primuloides* from the Himalayas is singularly obliging in this respect. Planted in a gritty scree sloping south, the rosettes of silver-haired leaves

push up 6-inch (15-cm) high stems, topped with clusters of deep pink flowers.

Aquilegia alpina

Even the aquilegia, normally so easy to grow, offers one or two temperamental high mountain forms. Most are no problem, except that they cross-pollinate with such liberal promiscuity that it is difficult to tell the legitimate from the illegitimate. So far I have never seen an ugly aquilegia. *Aquilegia alpina*, which I discovered growing wild in the Alps near Mont Cenis, has large blue and white flowers and grows about 12 inches (30 cm) high. Unfortunately, the only way to keep the true species is not to grow any other aquilegia within half a mile. *A. bertolonii*, at around 4 inches (10 cm) tall with bright blue flowers, is a gem best accommodated in a scree or hollow wall.

A. discolor is the species which gives me most pleasure. Dwarf in stature at 4 to 6 inches (10 to 15 cm) high with blue and white flowers over grey-green foliage, it is lovely, and easy to grow in most soils.

So often a large genus promises much yet gives little, and this is my experience with aster. Only one species measured up for cultivation in the rock garden, the European *Aster alpinus*. The tufted narrow leaves and large, purple, golden-centred daisy flowers on 6-inch (15-cm) stems are a feature in my limestone rock garden. There may be other good alpine species which so far I have not discovered.

Campanula allionii

The sun-loving campanula, popularly known as the 'Bell flower', offers so large a selection of species suitable for the rock garden that I am spoiled for choice. *Campanula allionii* from the European Alps grows best in a scree where it can spread by underground stems safe from marauding slugs. The large purple flowers open on stems which are only 3 inches (7 cm) high. The best-known is *C. carpatica* from the Bucegi mountains in the Transylvanian Alps of south-central Romania. It grows well in most soils and flowers profusely. I prefer named forms which grow no more than 6 inches (15 cm) high. The pick of the lot is *C. turbinata*, with dark blue, upturned bells carried one to a stem.

Cypripedium calceolus

Crocus vernus albiflorus

Again, as the slugs devour it avidly, the least vulnerable place is in a scree bed or hollow wall. Two plants of *C. cochlearifolia* have graced the hollow wall in front of my house for the last four years. The two have spread decorously by underground stems so that the white and blue colour forms intermingle. Then in June each year the bright green leaves are hidden by dancing legions of thimble-like bells on 2-inch (5-cm) stems. Only once have I seen the plant growing wild; it was in Austria where the flowers were less numerous but the back-cloth of the mountains was much more spectacular.

Crocus is so much a part of the spring scene – and then again of the autumn – that it would be difficult not to mention them if only briefly. *Crocus albiflorus* frequents the high alpine pastures from France to Yugoslavia. The flowers, white-flushed with blue, appear as the snow melts. The best-known of all the species crocus, *C. chrysanthus*, parent of so many hybrids, is a much better garden plant. Grow the corms in a well-drained soil in full sun. For further interest I raise fresh stock from seed, which takes three or four years from sowing to flowering.

For the autumn *C. speciosus* is the easiest to grow, even naturalising if planted in short, cropped turf. Its flowers are deep lilac blue.

Many cyclamen are not reliably hardy and must be grown indoors. *Cyclamen coum*, which comes from Eastern Europe, flowers in winter and spring in the garden and is perfectly hardy. The leaves of my plants are kidney-shaped, dark green above, red underneath. The shorter-petalled flowers on 2-inch (5-cm) stems are deep crimson or pink.

C. hederifolium is a great coloniser when suited by soil and situation. The leaves, beautifully marbled cream on green, are a feature right through the winter, and the large pink flowers open in the autumn before the leaves. Partial shade and a leaf-mould soil suit my plants satisfactorily.

I found the 'Lady Slipper' orchid, *Cypripedium calceolus*, growing in a boulder-strewn valley just on the edge of woodland in the Swiss Alps. To me it represents everything that I desire of a true alpine plant.

My first meeting with *Daphne cneorum* was in the Alps, on the Col d'Izoard, above the Durance valley, where it was growing in open glades, the fragrant pink flowers closely packed in terminal clusters only just protruding above the grass. The shrub grows in my rock garden with an annual top dressing of leaf mould, and it flowers in May. *D. striata* is similar, and grows in pockets of peat in stabilised scree at Lautaret. This species is not at all easy to cultivate in gardens, unlike *D. cneorum*.

Daphne cneorum

Dianthus is an integral part of the summer garden scene, so it is fortunate that there are so many which are suitable for growing with the other choice alpines. Most are lime tolerant; they prefer a place in the sun but are happy in a well-drained soil. *Dianthus alpinus* is a gem, making a prostrate mat of foliage with flowers the size of half crowns on 3-inch (7-cm) stems. The best forms have petals coloured rose to crimson. I always grow plants from seed unless tempted by an exceptionally good plant offered for sale in flower. *D. deltoides*, (The Maiden Pink), is too large for the small rock garden or scree at 8 inches (20 cm) high. The colours range from scarlet through pink to pure white. Far more acceptable is our own native 'Cheddar Pink', *D. gratianopolitanus*, which forms mats of low grey foliage, and has the loveliest, most sweetly scented pink flowers imaginable. Never growing much above 6 inches (15 cm), it makes good ground cover with some of the thymes. *D. pavonius (neglectus)* grows wild in lime-free soil and stars the turf with pink flowers at Lautaret. The backs of the petals are always buff-coloured, a characteristic passed on to its offspring.

Draba trails a long tail of two hundred or more species. Many are not particularly interesting, others moderately so, while a few are really choice. *Draba aizoides*, a rare native in Britain, is common in European mountains. The hard, tight, bristly rosettes of leaves and yellow flowers on 2-inch (5-cm) stems are a worth-while addition to a wall or scree garden.

There are some plants which charm and delight without being stridently beautiful, and the Mountain Avens, *Dryas octopetala*, is certainly one of these. The small, dark green, oak-shaped leaves show off the large white, short-stemmed flowers with a central boss of yellow stamens to good effect. This is a very desirable shrublet, which, unless it is kept in gritty soil, grows too well and never flowers.

Had I to choose one plant which encapsulates all the attributes of beauty and character which are possessed in varying degrees by so many of the alpine plants, *Eritrichium nanum* would gain the award. My first encounter was on a visit to Mont Cenis. I had spent the whole day looking at the choicest flowers that this richly endowed area affords – *Viola cenisia*, *Campanula cenisia*, *Saxifraga retusa*, to name but a few. I decided to climb higher, and there it was, the eritrichium, a dense, silver-haired cushion of sky-blue flowers with primrose-yellow centres. It is the complete, perfect, high-mountain plant, and is hopelessly difficult to cultivate even in an alpine house. The picture, like

Right: *Eritrichium nanum*, the 'King of the Alps'

vivid blue bosses on a shield of stone, is still clearly memorable.

Gentians have given me pleasure from when, while still a schoolboy, I first became aware of plants as individuals. *Gentiana verna* grows quite near to the school I attended. The deep, azure-blue flowers on short stems open in April to May. In the garden a humus-rich soil is the best, and the roots should be kept well watered in dry weather. *G. acaulis* is a friendly plant and grows in any rich, well-drained soil. I once used several dozen plants as an edging to a bed of HT roses, and they flowered splendidly. The brilliant, dark blue, trumpet-shaped flowers rise on short stalks from the dark green leaf rosettes. Both gentians will grow from divisions or seed.

Geraniums are another of the indispensables. Certainly *Geranium cinereum subcaulescens* with crimson, black-eyed flowers on 6 to 8 inch (15 to 20 cm) stems, is a very comely rock plant. Though the wood crane's-bill *G. sylvaticum* is a little robust for the rock garden proper, the cup-shaped bluish-purple flowers look well in association with dwarf shrubs planted on the outskirts. Height is around 15 inches (38 cm).

Of *Leontopodium alpinum* much has been said and sung; certainly, it is a well-loved, though by no means lovely, alpine plant. Grey-green leaves and white felted flowers will furnish a corner in full sun given average soil. It is easily raised from seed.

Linaria alpina from the scree slopes in the European Alps is more annual than perennial with me, but it perpetuates itself by means of seed without becoming a weed. Blue-grey leaves decked with violet, orange-throated flowers are the gardener's reward for a place in full sun on a well-drained soil.

The 'Alpine poppy', *Papaver alpinum*, is one of the most difficult plants to photograph, as even a fragment of breeze sets the flowers waving. I have seen the plants grow on steep scree slopes: tufts of fern-like foliage topped by flowers of white, pink, or yellow. My choice would be the variety *P. a. kerneri* with large yellow, paper-textured blooms in early summer. A pinch of seed scattered on gritty soil is all the effort required from the cultivator.

Below left: *Geranium sylvaticum*
Below: *Gentiana acaulis*

Linaria alpina

Papaver alpinum

I found the little *Polygala chamaebuxus* growing in moist peat soil on the same north slope as *Daphne cneorum*. Like a miniature box shrub in foliage, it grows in the hollow wall and is rarely if ever without a crop of yellow- and cream-lipped flowers. The form 'Grandiflora', with red and yellow blossom, is equally desirable. Though in nature polygala grows in partial shade, the hollow wall in my garden has proved acceptable. A neat, compact shrublet 4 inches (10 cm) high, massed with flowers, this makes a very creditable addition to any collection of rock plants. Propagation is by rooted offshoots lifted in May.

There are some shrubs which I consider essential when planting a simulated alpine landscape, and *Potentilla fruticosa* is one. I choose the dwarf forms which grow out rather than up. Full sun is needed for the yellow- or white-flowered varieties, partial shade for those with red or orange petals. Almost any soil will suit them except an oozing swamp. 'Longacre' and 'Goldfinger' are excellently dwarf and free flowering with me.

Primulas and rhododendrons deserve, even command, a chapter to themselves, and are dealt with elsewhere in this book.

When is an anemone not an anemone? The answer seems to be, when the botanists decree it shall be pulsatilla. I still think of pulsatilla as anemone or 'Windflowers', though this is now incorrect. *Pulsatilla alpina* with white flowers and *P. a. apiifolia* with rich yellow flowers are frequenters of the alpine meadows. Both grow well in acid or alkaline soil, but at 18 or 24 inches (46 or 51 cm) high are too tall for the rock garden proper. Grow the

plants from seed, and prick them off into pots, for they do hate root disturbance at any stage.

Saxifraga oppositifolia

The sight vivid in memory of *P. alpina* in full bloom across a sloping hillside with snow-capped mountains behind, almost persuades me that this and not eritrichium is the 'King of the Alps'. The flowers, cupped in a filigree of fern-like foliage, are white with golden stamens, the outer sepals bewhiskered with silky gold and purple hairs. In seconds the colour changes from pink to gold to opal white – a delightful spring picture. I have never seen the same qualities reflected in cultivation, though *P. vernalis* is not hard to grow in humus-rich soil.

Ranunculus glacialis resists all attempts to wean it from mountain slope to garden. In nature the wide-spreading tufts of grey-green leaves, like those of an aconite, spread far and wide, often most luxuriantly in very wet but obviously free-draining soil beside mountain tarns. The very large, pure white, golden-centred flowers deepen with age to rose-red. Respect slowly replaces covetousness for this most determined mountaineer.

Saxifraga 'Valerie Finnis'

One of the largest families, Saxifraga, is also sufficiently diverse in character to warrant further division into sub-sections. Some grow in rock crevices on sheer cliff faces, others ribbon the stones with bands of scarlet along the mountain streams. The Kabschia section form tight mounds of attractively rounded rosettes of foliage. Brightly coloured, short-stemmed flowers appear in early spring. The hollow wall or very gritty scree is suitable, though pot culture in the alpine house is even better.

The Euaizoonia section contains all those species with silvered foliage. Long branching panicles of white flowers, spotted pink or red, are a feature in spring. I grow them in the crevices or between rocks of weathered limestone. Saxifraga

Sempervivum tectorum var. alpinum

section Porphyrion includes two easy-to-grow gems in *S. oppositifolia* and *S. retusa*. Both I found growing wild, either along the edge of glacial streams or the verges of mountain pools. *S. oppositifolia* makes a creeping mat of foliage starred with red-purple flowers in April to May. *S. retusa* is neater and more congested, with deeper red flowers. Both grow in lime-free scree with extra peat added, and a large stone alongside to keep the roots cool.

Sempervivums always give me the impression that they can live on fresh air and water. They grow quite luxuriantly on stone slate house roofs. There are fifty or so species and numerous hybrids, most of which are easy to grow in well-drained soil providing humus is added. Wall crevices, cracks between rocks, even the edge of a gravel path will suit. I remember seeing *Sempervivum tectorum var. alpinum* growing wild on a railway embankment in the Swiss Alps. *S. arachnoideum*, the 'Cobweb houseleek', is most decorative; the network of silver hairs over the rosettes of leaves are a characteristic, and in due season pink flowers add to the charm of this species.

In the high alpine scrubland, seeming to erupt through the melting snow, *Soldanella alpina* makes the most of early spring sunshine. Deep blue flowers, bell-shaped and fringed, nodding over rounded dark green leaves make the climb to discover them a small toll to pay. My search for *S. montana* was never rewarded, so instead I grow the plant in my garden. It is larger in all its parts than *S. alpina*; the deep blue, fringed bells sway to every breeze on 6-inch (15-cm) stems.

Soldanella alpina

Alpine plants offer so many alluring fields of study that it is easy to become so engrossed in their cultivation that all other avenues of gardening are looked on as unworthy of attention.

2
Tulips

The story of the tulip is one of the brightest patterns woven into the historical tapestry of garden plants. Fortunately, the early history of the tulip is well documented, which is not surprising, and the text is fascinating to read.

As a species, tulips occur naturally in Europe, North Africa, and through to West and Central Asia, so the majority are hardy enough to be grown outdoors in the British Isles. The name Tulipa is derived from 'tuliban', a Persian or Turkish word meaning a turban. Though the splendidly colourful hybrid tulips dominate the garden scene, the species from which they have been developed are equally worthy of consideration. Their beauty, less garish, persuades rather than commands. The tulip appears to have been brought to this country some time in the last quarter of the sixteenth century. Certainly, there are records of tulip bulbs being grown in Antwerp in 1562, though they had been cultivated as a garden flower in Turkey probably from the beginning of the century. In the year 1554 an ambassador to the court of Suleiman the Magnificent saw tulips growing, almost certainly hybrids. Seeds were delivered to Vienna, and the first recorded illustration of the flower was made in 1561. This bloom, a cultivated hybrid which was first thought to be a species, *Tulipa gesneriana*, could be termed the progenitor of all modern tulips.

Carolus Clusius (Jules Charles de l'Ecluse), prefect of the Royal Medicinal Garden, Prague, received some of the first seeds, and, interestingly he was the one to mention the first double tulip. Clusius continued working with tulips following his appointment as Professor of Botany in Leiden. Who could have foreseen in the year 1600, while Clusius and, no doubt, other like-minded gardeners were raising bulbs from seed and observing the flowers, that in thirty years fortunes would be made, then lost again, over the sale of bulbs? The 1630s saw such an explosion of interest in the newest colour forms that bulbs changed hands for hundreds of pounds each. It is hard to imagine the tulip, familiar garden flower that it is, as an object of greedy speculation. Eventually 'Tulipomania', as it was called, reached a fever pitch until, in 1637, the bottom fell out of the market, halting further speculation in bulb trading. Thousands of people must have been ruined when the market collapsed; fortunately

Tulipa fosteriana 'Cantata'

the tulip survived to become one of Holland's major export industries. Only recently has the study of virus diseases revealed that the valued and much sought after striped and variously coloured blooms of the seventeenth century were not a product of the hybridiser's art; their characteristics were, and still are, caused by virus infection.

The glory and variety of colour which tulips possess, their versatility, offering species suitable for the rock garden, window box, and massed bedding schemes, have assured for them a secure place in the gardener's affection and esteem for almost four hundred years. During that time there have been further peaks of interest. In the 1850s catalogues listed over a thousand varieties, with several of the newest introductions priced at £100 each. There is a record of single bulbs being sold in Holland

during the same period for over £600. Fortunately, the present-day price per bulb enables the interested gardener to grow tulips without having to mortgage the house in order to pay for the indulgence. Modern nursery catalogues issue lists of varieties as extensive as those of the mid-nineteenth century, and in gardening terms the lists are divided into sections.

The group known as the 'Single Early' tulips offers a wide range of colours and is excellent for bedding work. They grow from 14 to 20 inches (35 to 50 cm), which is low enough to prevent them from being decapitated by boisterous spring winds. Because they flower early they are ready for lifting in good time, and the soil can be prepared for planting with summer bedding. Though it is not possible to mention more than a few varieties, of those I have grown 'Keizerskroon' with large red blooms edged with yellow, carried on 14-inch (35-cm) stems, has always proved satisfactory. Indeed, any garden plant would need to be possessed of special merit still to be listed three hundred years after being introduced, for 'Keizerskroon' is said to date from 1681. Another variety which I find most agreeable is 'Couleur Cardinal', which again grows only 14 inches (35 cm) high, with dark red blooms faintly tinged with purple on the outside; it is one of the most weather-resistant tulips I have tried.

For early flowering in pots, the lovely, golden-orange-petalled 'General de Wet' or the crisper yellow 'Bellona' will often be showing colour in February. 'Bellona' distils a pleasant fragrance, a quality not usually associated with tulips.

'Double Early' tulips express a quite different character. The multiplication of the petals is acknowledged in the descriptive popular name, 'Paeony-flowered tulip'. All the varieties I have

Above: *Tulipa* 'Bellona'

Top right: *Tulipa* 'Peach Blossom'
Below right: *Tulipa* 'Duc Van Tol'

grown are short stemmed, which makes them excellent material for use in patio tubs and window boxes. Two of the Double Early varieties proved useful for early colour in a cold greenhouse when grown in pots. Bulbs of the rich scarlet-flowered 'Carlton' and the equally impressive buttercup-yellow 'Hytuna' were potted up in peat-based compost in October. The pots were plunged outdoors until late December before being moved into the unheated greenhouse. Both varieties were in full bloom during March, and all their beauty could be enjoyed as they were not sullied by the weather. They can, of course, be planted outdoors in October or November to flower at the normal time in April. For those who enjoy a composed association I would recommend the pink blooms of 'Peach Blossom' mixed with the dark blue of *Scilla* 'Spring Beauty'.

Several crosses have been made between the original groups to produce varieties which flower at a time roughly between those of the two parents. 'Mendel' tulips arrived as a result of a cross between the very early-blooming 'Duc Van Tol' and several Darwin tulips. The combination resulted in new varieties like 'Van der Eerden', a bright crimson-red, which lends itself very well to pot cultivation indoors; and the strikingly tinted 'Orange Wonder' in shades of bronze, scarlet, and orange. Colour combinations of this degree need careful handling in the

Above: *Tulipa* 'Duc Van Tol Aurora'

Tulipa 'Peerless Pink'

Top: *Tulipa* 'Pink Supreme'
Above: *Tulipa* 'Carnova'

garden design, with the cool blue of forget-me-not or muscari to act as a soothing undertone.

The Triumph tulips were the produce of a pollen exchange between the Darwin group and the more vigorous-growing Single Early tulips. Hybrid vigour possibly explains the strong sturdy stems and longer-lasting flowers which make Triumph varieties such good cut flowers. Of those I have tried 'Preludium' is well worth a place, the petals deep rose fading gradually to pure white at the base. 'Reforma', sulphur-yellow, and 'Peerless Pink' flushed with mauve, are also sturdy and long lasting in bloom. *T.* 'Marco Polo' is a newer variety with a crimson colour flushed with yellow.

Tall-growing tulips are breath-takingly beautiful when massed in beds, and are featured in parks department displays throughout the British Isles. Darwin tulips 'Bleu Aimable', lavender-mauve, 'Pink Supreme', deep pink, and the unusual 'Carnova' are impressive. Darwin hybrids such as these are produced by crossing the brilliant scarlet-flowered species *T. fosteriana* with the vigorous Darwins to produce tall plants with large flowers so vividly coloured that the very air around the area of the garden in which they are growing seems warmed by the display. 'Holland's Glorie', with large, orange-red blooms grows 24 inches (61 cm) high, and 'Red Matador' is so aggressively scarlet that only against the dark background of a conifer hedge can its quality be fully appreciated. As material for floral decoration, the regal magnificence of the tulip 'Queen Wilhelmina' is quite superb. Tall at nearly 30 inches (76 cm), the petals, orange-scarlet paling at the edges, are in fact too large in the isolation of a bedding display, but most effective planted in groups down a shrub or herbaceous border.

For some years I grew a mixture of the Rembrandt varieties in a bed which included a fine specimen of the grey-leaved weeping pear, *Pyrus salicifolia* 'Pendula'. I never did adjust to the Joseph's-coat pattern produced by the multi-coloured, flaked, striped, and feathered petals. Named varieties enable the colour scheme to be adjusted and modulated to a level I find more acceptable. In practice, Rembrandts excite the interest of flower arrangers more than the enthusiasm of gardeners.

Cottage or May-flowering tulips are very hard to categorise. In catalogues it is not unusual to find a variety listed under Darwin in one grower's list, and under Cottage in another. So far as I can discover, in the early part of the nineteenth century a group of enthusiasts collected together the late-flowering tulips from established colonies existing in the gardens of that period, and used the best as breeding stock. They are strong growing, with rounded flowers carried on stems up to 30 inches (76 cm) high. 'Golden Harvest', a deep lemon, is earlier-flowering than most of the others, and is usually in colour by late April. 'Greenland', with green-tinged petals edged with pink, is a popular variety for use in floral arrangements. 'Sweet Harmony' is also useful for cutting; the lemon-yellow flowers with a white margin stand for a long time in floral arrangements. A newer variety, 'Burgundy Lace', is an attractive scarlet-red.

Though the Lily-flowered varieties bloom at the same time as, and are often grouped with, Cottage tulips, in flower shape

Tulipa 'Greenland'

Above: *Tulipa* 'Maytime'
Right: *Tulipa* 'Mariette'

they are quite distinct. Long, narrow-waisted blooms with reflexing petals present a graceful appearance in contrast to the ovoid flowers of other May-flowering varieties. Usually they are shorter in stature, the stem length ranging between 15 and 24 inches (38 and 61 cm). 'Mariette', with deep pink, emphatically recurved petals, grows up to 20 inches (51 cm) high. 'Maytime', lilac with a white edge, and 'West Point', yellow, are shorter and look well when grouped together.

'Elizabeth Arden' is a variety of the Darwin hybrid type which I first planted twenty-six years ago. The petals are coloured rose-violet on the outside with a salmon-rose interior – an improbable combination which proves most effective.

For me Parrot tulips are an acquired taste, the clusters of twisted and fringed petals, often measuring 10 inches (25 cm) across, look more like the flowers of the paeony. A massed planting in full bloom on a warm May day is spectacular. 'Orange Favourite', 'Faraday', 'Texas Flame', 'Flaming Parrot', and 'Black Parrot' would serve as an introductory planting.

The bulbs to be grown outdoors are best planted in late October or November – a most inhospitable time of year, it would seem, but earlier planting means that the bulbs are too soon into growth, which exposes the foliage and flower buds to frost. On heavy soils 4 inches (10 cm) will be sufficiently deep to bury the bulbs; lighter soils encourage deeper planting, to 6 or 8 inches (15 or 20 cm) below the surface. The distance apart varies according to whether the bulbs are used in a formal bedding

Top left: *Tulipa* 'Texas Flame'
Below left: *Tulipa* 'Orange Favourite'
Right: *Tulipa* 'Flaming Parrot'

scheme or to achieve a random effect. For formal work 4 to 6 inches (10 to 15 cm) apart according to variety is adequate.

Any good garden soil which is well drained and has not been freshly manured will grow tulips well. Where the soil condition needs improving, work in a dressing of well-rotted compost or moist peat after lifting out summer bedding plants in late September. As tulips thrive best in an alkaline soil, provision should be made for this if the soil is at all acid in reaction by dressing the surface with chalk or ground limestone either before or, as I have often done, after planting, particularly if the soil is on the heavy side of medium texture.

Though the tulip species and the hybrids produced from them are less assertive than the Darwin, Triumph, and other bedding varieties, they are, particularly for the owners of small gardens, of equal value. They are beautiful in flower, adaptable in cultivation indoors or for planting outdoors in the rock garden, borders, patios, or window boxes. There are some – *Tulipa tarda* is an example in my own garden – which have spread into quite sizeable colonies over the years. Bulbs planted in a well-drained soil will add another colour dimension to the garden scene in spring. I leave some of the species in the ground all the year round, maintaining the vigour of the bulbs by regular feeding with bone meal and compost top dressing.

Unless seed is needed for raising new stock I take off the flower heads as petals fall. The leaves are not cleared away until they wither and part easily from the bulbs.

One of the most popular species is the water-lily tulip, *T. kaufmanniana*, which combines a very compact habit with large, brilliantly coloured flowers. Indeed, so many hybrids have been introduced from crosses between this species with *T. fosteriana* and the ever-productive *T. greigii*, that the choice is so wide as to be bewildering. In the type species, *T. kaufmanniana* grows only about 6 inches (15 cm) high. The creamy-yellow flower is tinged pink on the outside and rises out of a basal rosette of grey-green

leaves very early in spring. Of the varieties I have grown 'Shakespeare', the flowers a mixture of salmon, apricot, and orange on 5-inch (13-cm) high stems, are reliable and pleasantly unusual. 'Stresa', yellow flushed with red, and 'Heart's Delight' a pinky white flushed with red, will bring colour to any garden on a cold spring day.

In spite of several attempts I cannot be certain that the bulbs purchased as *T. fosteriana* were the true species. Though the flower colour, scarlet with a yellow-edged basal blotch, is faithfully produced in each case, the height varies from a modest 7 inches (18 cm) in one group to an extreme 18 inches (46 cm) in another. Flower size shows a similar wide variation. Of the hybrids I would choose 'Princeps', vivid red blooms on 8-inch

Tulipa kaufmanniana 'Heart's Delight'

Below left: *Tulipa kaufmanniana* 'Shakespeare'
Below: *Tulipa kaufmanniana* 'Stresa'

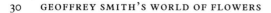

Tulipa fosteriana 'Cantata'

(20-cm) stems, or 'Cantata', whose bright scarlet petals are narrowly reflexed and beautifully shaped.

T. greigii has such attractively marked leaves that it would almost be worth including as a foliage plant. The species and all the varieties I have grown derived from it have leaves which are veined with maroon or purple-brown. Brilliantly coloured flowers open on short stems during April and early May. Though they are dwarf enough to be accommodated in the rock garden, I prefer to use these vivid flowers in massed bedding, tubs, or window boxes. Given free choice of all the varieties on offer, I would select 'Red Riding Hood' with scarlet-red petals, which I grow alongside an elaeagnus with golden leaves to achieve an effect which verges on the violent. The variety 'Dreamboat' has a

Tulipa greigii 'Red Hiding Hood'

delightful colour combination, each petal with an amber-yellow ground colour shaded with red.

The species tulips offer such a wealth of beauty and interest that it is hard to resist becoming a collector. There are some which, like the tiny *T. pulchella*, will succeed only in northern gardens when grown in pots. Violet-red flowers on 4- to 6-inch (10- to 15-cm) stems nestle close amongst the leaves in March. Others are more robust, sensibly flowering when there is promise if not an actuality of spring, and so can be safely planted outdoors. *T. clusiana* (lady tulip) grows 12 inches (30 cm) high, and is white with the three outer petals carrying a bold cherry-red stripe. I grow this tulip in company with forget-me-nots and a dark-green-foliaged dwarf conifer, so that the flowers are shown in bold contrast. *T. batalinii* looks so primly modest that I like to see it in association with cottage garden flowers – pinks, pansy, and the smoky-grey foliage of 'Lad's love'. Both the type species *T. batalinii* and the hybrid 'Bronze Charm' are very compact-growing, being only 4 to 6 inches (10 to 15 cm) high. The former has lovely soft-yellow flowers; the hybrid has blossoms which vary between bronze and apricot. Mention must be made here of our own native tulip, *T. sylvestris*, still to be found growing wild in isolated pockets of the British Isles, and in cultivation at the Cambridge Botanic Gardens.

Tulipa pulchella 'Humilus'

Tulipa sylvestris

Tulipa praestans 'Fusilier'

T. *praestans* is unusual in that instead of one flower, several orange-scarlet blooms are carried on a 12-inch (30-cm) stem. Both the species and hybrids – of which 'Fusilier' would be my choice – are good value as they do not need to be lifted each year. One group that I have planted among dwarf shrubs in the rock garden has flowered very creditably for the last four years.

The most perennial species I have grown is a native of Russia, T. *tarda*, illustrated on the cover of this book. This is so well suited by soil and climate that it has spread self-sown seedlings into a bed of crocus nearby. The leaf rosettes lie flat to support clusters of flowers which are white with a central yellow eye. Growing to about 5 inches (13 cm) high, they can be comfortably accommodated on the outskirts of the rock garden.

Similar in character to T. *tarda*, the Iranian species T. *urumiensis* with star-shaped yellow flowers has also proved suitable in an alpine context. The petals are yellow-stained bronze, opening to show deeper yellow anthers. T. *biflora* is another attractive species. A native of Russia, it has pale green leaves, and each stem bears three to five white flowers with a yellow eye in early spring. Not spectacular, just quietly and obligingly pleasant.

Species tulips in no way compete with the large-flowered garden hybrids. There is a place for both even in the smaller garden context. The large-flowered garden hybrids are best lifted when the foliage has withered. After being dried off they can then be cleaned of soil or other debris before being stored until required for replanting in autumn. I leave species tulips in the ground without disturbance; colonies which die out under this treatment can be replaced at reasonable cost.

Tulipa batalinii 'Bronze Charm'

3
Rhododendrons

Rhododendrons present a bewildering array to the novice gardener as he scans the list of species and varieties available. There are somewhere between seven hundred and a thousand species, showing such a marked difference in character that at times it is hard to accept that they belong to the same genus. To compare a tiny, mat-forming midget only an inch or two (2·5 or 5 cm) high with a forest tree towering 40 feet (12 m) above one's head requires a mental dexterity that only a specialist can acquire. Fortunately, the amateur need not become embroiled in the finer chemical or botanical details that separate one species from another. Though it is nice to know that the genus *Rhododendron* subdivides into groups and series, it is information essential only to the botanist or specialist grower.

The rhododendron story is fascinating, beginning with the plant explorers who at considerable personal risk collected plants or seed in China, Tibet, India, Burma, and Nepal. Their names are firmly established in garden history: Sir Joseph Hooker, Robert Fortune, George Forrest, and the French missionaries Abbé Delavay and Père David. There is no epitaph more worthy or enduring than the species named after them.

There is one limitation which prevents all who would from growing rhododendrons. A lime-free soil is essential. Some rhododendrons can be persuaded by generous mulches of peat and frequent applications of trace elements to grow in an alkaline soil, but they never really thrive. Given an acid soil, plenty of moisture, and shelter from cold winds, they are unsurpassed in beauty of flower, or infinite variety of form and foliage. Shelter from cold wind is a prime requirement for all Asiatic rhododendrons except the small-leafed species (*Lepidote*) which clothe the mountains above the highest level of tree growth – between 10 000 and 15 000 feet (3 000 and 4 600 m).

Experience has shown that the majority of species rhododendrons are quite well able to stand the severest winter likely to be inflicted on the British Isles, providing the cold is unbroken. Indeed, under natural conditions they are dormant because of the severe weather for six or seven months of the year. Conditions in the average winter here are very different, with long periods of mild weather which cause flower buds to put down

A delightful woodland setting for rhododendrons at Exbury Gardens, near Southampton

their protecting scales and start to open prematurely, only to be killed by a sudden bleak frost. Alternate freeze and thaw can continue even into May, killing the current year's blooms and blackening the young growth, which also destroys prospects for the following season.

The ideal site on which to grow rhododendrons would be in open glades in woodland, consisting of deep-rooted trees like oak. Other trees are suitable only if they do not compete for moisture and food with the shallow, surface-rooting rhododendron. The smaller-leafed species are better suited in a more open position, associating well with low-growing heathers and dwarf conifers. I prepare the soil in advance of planting by working in heavy dressings of moist peat, leaf mould, or well-rotted manure. This results in the moist, almost spongy root run in which all ericaceous plants revel. When planting, it is important to make certain that the top of the root ball is level with the soil surface.

To ensure against its drying out, finish off with a 2-inch (5-cm) covering of peat or leaf mould. Deep planting can kill even healthy rhododendrons; the high planting and peat mulch are the best safeguards. The best time to plant is in April to May when growth is active during periods of warm, moist weather. I have moved plants in full bloom, kept them well-watered afterwards without their losing a single leaf.

The first species to be introduced and recorded were *R. hirsutum* and *R. ferrugineum* from the European Alps. *R. hirsutum* arrived first – a small shrub with clusters of tubular flowers opening in June. Certainly, John Tradescant was growing this species in his garden in the mid-seventeenth century. Not until nearly a hundred years later is there any mention of *R. ferrugineum* being in cultivation. Popularly known as the Alpine rose, the flowers are tubular, rose-crimson, opening in tight trusses during June.

In 1736 the first of several species arrived from America, to be closely followed in 1763 by what most people regard as the archetypal rhododendron, the ubiquitous *R. ponticum* from Armenia and Asia Minor. Now it is so well naturalised as to be a weed nuisance in forestry plantations. It is useful as an informal hedge and will make, in time, a large shrub 15 feet (4·6 m) high. The flower colour varies from lilac-pink to mauve. In the past it has often been used as a root-stock on which to graft scions of named varieties. Occasionally the scion dies, and the root-stock survives to establish yet another colony of common *ponticum*.

Early in the nineteenth century two species were discovered. *R. caucasicum*, from the mountain of that name in the Caucasus, was found growing virtually on the snow line. Six years later the second species, *R. catawbiense*, was introduced from the Allegheny mountains in the United States of America. The material was at hand for the plant breeder to work with, and the result was several notable hardy hybrids. The best-known is the early-flowering 'Christmas Cheer', densely compact in growth with pink blossoms fading to white.

Rhododendron ponticum

Rhododendron arboreum

Not until the advent of *R. arboreum* in the early nineteenth century did it become possible to produce the scarlet and vivid crimson varieties which are such an illuminating feature of our woodlands and gardens. *R. arboreum* was the first Himalayan species to be introduced. The blood-red flowers open during the coldest months of the year in favoured localities, the first colour shows in January, so the display is frequently ruined by frost. I have seen specimens 30 feet (9 m) high laden down with globular heads of red-petalled flowers glowing in March sunshine, making the whole tree a vibrant cone of colour.

Fascinating though the natural species are, it is the hybrids which have ensured the rhododendron's continuing popularity as a garden rather than a park or woodland shrub. The crossing of the red *R. arboreum* on to the old *R. catawbiense* and *R. ponticum* hybrids really heralded the birth of the vast range of garden hybrid rhododendrons available today. All this was only a first tentative step, for it merely pre-empted the mass introduc-

Rhododendron falconeri

tion of new species from the Himalayas, which began with Sir
Joseph Hooker's expedition in 1848. Like anyone else who grows
rhododendrons for any length of time, I have my favourites, and
it is surprising how many are contained in the forty-three species
collected by Hooker during the two years of the expedition –
species of such quality that they alone would have raised the
status of the genus as garden plants to share pride of place with
the rose.

The large-leafed *R. falconeri*, with huge trusses of creamy-
white flowers each printed with a stain of purple on the throat,
must have taken the gardening world by storm when it bloomed
for the first time. Like all the large-leafed species, it needs the
shelter provided by a woodland glade. Another of the Hooker
introductions, *R. ciliatum*, which grows wild on steep mountain
slopes if the soil is moist enough, or along the margins of streams,

Rhododendron thomsonii

at up to 12 000 feet (3 600 m) in the Sino-Himalayas, is a complete contrast to *R. falconeri*. This species grows to only 3 or 4 feet (0·9 or 1·2 m) high with 3-inch-long (8-cm) leaves fringed with hair, and bell-shaped flowers of a delicate shell-pink. The buds start to break early, and year after year the flowers on my plants were blackened by frost. Eventually, in a kill-or-cure treatment I moved the plants out into an open north-facing border. Here growth is compact, and most years the flowers open late enough to escape the frost.

R. thomsonii with scarlet petals so textured that they present a waxed appearance, and lovely glaucous grey-blue foliage is, undoubtedly, pleasing though requiring woodland conditions to achieve full potential. Indeed, the list reads like *Who's Who*; with the yellow *R. campylocarpum* and the superb but tender *R. griffithianum* to tempt the appetite it is not surprising that in what now seems to be excessive zeal gardeners rushed to plant them. Ignorance of the ultimate height or spread of the species being planted should impose restraint, or within a very short time – as happened in so many newly created rhododendron gardens – the plants become overcrowded so that all the beauty of form is lost. Though *R. griffithianum* is not amongst the hardiest species, this did not prevent it being used to cross-pollinate other species. Indeed, a hybrid of *R. griffithianum* crossed with a hybrid of that patriarchal *R. arboreum* produced one of the most admired hybrids ever, the iron-constitutioned 'Pink Pearly'. *R. ciliatum* is also parent to a noteworthy hybrid in the early-flowering *R. × praecox*, whose rose-purple flowers open in March, adding a contrast to the predominantly yellow theme of that season.

Of all the plant hunters, George Forrest is the one to whom gardeners owe the greatest debt. The total number of plants he collected amounted to over thirty thousand: a prodigious achievement when related to the difficult terrain he was working in, the primitive conditions he had to live under, and the archaic transport available, both for himself and the dispatch of the plants from China to this country. The list of rhododendrons Forrest discovered in the Tali mountains of north-west Yunnan reveals the extent of his contribution to our knowledge of the genus. Particularly valuable were the many alpine dwarf species of rhododendrons which he imported. Like all plants of modest stature they exercise a peculiar fascination. In practical terms, twenty dwarf species or hybrids can be accommodated in the area occupied by one mature, taller-growing species which frequently covers an area 150 feet (46 m) in circumference. The dwarf species will grow in open situations, making themselves at home in rock or heather garden in conditions which would desiccate the large-leafed rhododendrons. *R. forrestii*, the species which bears his name, forms a mat of foliage only an inch or two (2·5 to 5 cm) high. The large, bell-shaped flowers borne in pairs are bright scarlet. Even in moist soil and shade, which it prefers, my plant rarely flowers. In this event a hybrid between *R. forrestii repens* and the tender but eminently desirable *R. griersonianum* is to be preferred. This hybrid, called 'Elizabeth', is of dwarf habit; the clustered heads of rich-red flowers open in April.

Rhododendron augustinii in the
Royal Botanic Garden, Edinburgh

Forrest, amongst others, also imported the dwarf yellow-flowered, aromatic-leafed *R. sargentianum*. This forms a lovely contrast to the even more compact, deep purple-rose blossoms of a species he introduced in 1910 called, very aptly, '*R. prostratum*'. So then the number of species grew in quantity and in variety of foliage and flower, surely enough to fill every possible situation or need which our gardens afford.

What, in fact, did happen was that anyone and everyone who grew rhododendrons began to cross-pollinate, so that new hybrids were manufactured in such numbers that muddle and confusion were inevitable. To make any sort of gardening sense, hybridisation must be embarked upon with a specific purpose in mind. To do this parents are carefully selected for qualities of leaf, flower, hardiness, or habit of growth. One is designated as the female or seed parent. When the flowers are still immature they are enclosed in a muslin bag to exclude completely insects which could cross-fertilise the flower prematurely. When the petals expand, the stamens (or male organs) are removed with a pair of nail tweezers, which prevents self-pollination of the flower. When the stigma becomes sticky – a sure sign of maturity for pollination – anthers from the chosen male parent which are shedding pollen are rubbed over the stigma of the female. The muslin bag is kept in place until it is obvious that the cross has taken. I always make a note of the exact parentage – male and female – and the date the cross was made. Hybrids are not acceptable without a birth certificate, so to speak. The seed capsules take anything up to ten months before the case starts to open at the tip, indicating that the seeds are ready for dispersal. I harvest the capsules, then leave them on saucers or newspapers until the seeds drop out.

For sowing, a half pot 4 or 5 inches (10 or 13 cm) in diameter will do very well. The compost I have found suitable is 2 parts sieved peat, 1 part sharp lime-free sand. Fill the pot with the mixture to within half an inch (1·2 cm) of the rim. A piece of zinc or broken pot over the drainage hole is advisable, though not essential. Firm the compost lightly with a pot press, then sow the seed thinly over the surface. Keep well-watered by plunging the pot up to the rim in rain-water – unlike tap-water this is sure to be lime-free. I protect the pots with butter muslin at all stages, before and after germination, to prevent scorching of the leaves. The seedlings are grown on for a year, or even two years, before being pricked off into an ericaceous compost for growing on.

Making a choice from the thousands of different species and varieties available is not easy, even with thirty years' experience. The following are good garden value, starting first with the species – though it must be admitted that they lack the adaptability of the hybrids. *R. augustinii* is a tall-growing shrub with small leaves; the best forms have deep blue flowers which open in late April to May. It is a good, quick-growing species which looks particularly pleasing in patterned shade. It is easily propagated by means of cuttings made from young growths. These are taken in July into a rooting compost of 2 parts lime-free sand and 1 part peat. *R. orbiculare* is a dense evergreen shrub

Top left: *Rhododendron orbiculare*
Below left: *Rhododendron wardii*

with clusters of pink flowers borne in April to May. *R. wardii* is one of the most outstanding yellow-flowered species to be introduced from China. It is sufficiently attractive to warrant a sheltered corner of a large garden. *R. vernicosum* is one of George Forrest's introductions still to be found growing in the Royal Botanic Garden, Edinburgh. The young buds are pink, and the white flowers are at their best in early May. *R. cinnabarinum* is a medium-sized shrub in all the forms available; a most beautiful and desirable decoration for the garden. The flowers are pendant tubes of bright cinnabar-red. An added charm is revealed in the blue-green of the young unfolding leaves. *R. haematodes* ranks amongst the pick of Chinese rhododendrons, with its neat, compact growth and dark green leaves, which are covered on the undersides with fox-red, felt-like hairs called indumentum. This character, exhibited by certain species, gives them a perennial beauty. In May to June *R. haematodes* displays scarlet-crimson, bell-shaped flowers. It is certainly, one of George Forrest's most praiseworthy introductions. In my last garden a bush had grown only 30 inches (76 cm) high by 36 inches (91 cm) across in twenty years. *R. impeditum*, one of the dwarf alpine shrublets at most 1 foot (30 cm) high, is a gem of the genus. Silvered foliage sets off the dark blue flowers. *R. pemakoense* is another very handsome dwarf alpine shrub. Of the two forms I have grown one spread by suckers. This is a very free-flowering little species; in April the 1-foot-high (30-cm) dome of leaves disappears under a screen of lilac-pink blooms. *R. prostratum* creeps along close to the ground, and is splendid for furnishing the north face of the rock garden. The flowers, which open almost flat, are crimson with darker spots.

Right: *Rhododendron cinnabarinum*

Above:
Rhododendron spinuliferum
Above right:
Rhododendron williamsianum
Right:
Rhododendron sinogrande

Below:
Rhododendron 'Curlew'
Below right:
Rhododendron fastigiatum

Rhododendron yakushimanum

An unnamed rhododendron seedling

There are several forms of the variable species *R. racemosum*. The best is the one originally collected by George Forrest known as 'Forrest's Dwarf'. The rufous-red branchlets wreathed in bright pink flowers are fit adornment for the most choice rock or shrub garden. *R. russatum* has received enough awards, including that of 'Garden Merit' from the Royal Horticultural Society in 1938, to warrant inclusion for the first-rate garden plant that it is. It grows about 3 feet (0·9 m) high; the foliage has a copper tint in early spring; and the flowers are deep violet with white shading in the throat. *R. williamsianum* has rounded leaves, bronze young growth, and beautifully formed pink, bell-shaped flowers. A sheltered position is advisable, as the buds show colour early and are liable to be frosted.

There are many more species. The magnificent-leafed *R. sinogrande, basilicum* and others of similar character are specialist plants, achieving their full beauty in the moister, warmer gardens of the west coast. An unusual looking species is *R. spinuliferum* which was flowering well in May at Wakehurst Gardens in Sussex. However, had I to choose just one species from the list, it would be, undoubtedly, *R. yakushimanum*. Found growing only on the mountain slopes of Yakushima Island, Japan, this really is a choice shrub for small or large garden. Over several years it will grow into a dome-shaped bush just 3 to 4 feet (0·9 to 1·2 m) high. Mature leaves are dark, glossy green above and brown-felted below. Young growths are silvered-grey suede in texture. Apple-blossom pink in bud, the flowers open in May and fade to white with age.

Dwarf rhododendrons are very popular in small gardens where space is at a premium. A favourite of mine is *R. fastigiatum* which grows to a height of 3 feet (0·9 m) and has a spread of 2 feet (60 m). The light-purple flowers open in April, and it makes an excellent grouping with heathers. Amongst the dwarf hybrids *R.* 'Pink Drift' flowers profusely in early May, whilst *R.* 'Curlew' is not only a compact plant ideal for the rock garden, but is often used as a parent for new varieties. More and more new varieties are arriving to join old established ones. Even as yet unnamed

Rhododendron luteum

seedlings seem to have that special quality which make the
rhododendrons such popular garden shrubs.

Azaleas are very much a part of the family, so closely akin that
they are now listed as rhododendrons. They require the same
cultivation, though the majority of deciduous varieties will
flower well in full sun so long as the soil is moist. One fully-hardy
hybrid is R. 'Palestrina'. This has white flowers with a trace of
green, and is a mass of bloom at Exbury Gardens in early May.
There is a certain doubt about the hardiness of R. *schlippenbachii*
which my experience denies – it is a very desirable garden plant.
The rose pink, saucer-shaped flowers open on naked branches, to
be followed by foliage which is purple-tinged when young. In the
autumn the leaves turn crimson and gold before being shed.

The most popular of this group is the 'Honeysuckle azalea',
R. *luteum* – my choice if I were allowed only one species to grow
with R. *yakushimanum*. The primrose-yellow, fragrant flowers
are a feature in May; then in October the leaves turn vivid shades
of orange, red, and purple. Brilliant autumn colour is a feature of
many deciduous azaleas.

All the species rhododendrons can be raised from seed sown
in suitable lime-free compost – either the 2 parts peat, 1 part sand
previously described, or the ericaceous mixture on sale in the

Azaleas in all their glory
at Exbury Gardens

garden shops. Seed saved from open-pollinated species may have been crossed with a different species or hybrid, so will not grow into an exact replica of the parent.

Small-leafed rhododendron, including the azaleas, will grow from cuttings made of semi-ripe young growth taken in July to August. All rhododendrons can be layered by means of branches which grow low enough to be pegged down into a mixture of peat and sand. Make a cut on the underside of the branch, halfway through and about 2 to 3 inches (5 to 8 cm) long. I pop a piece of sphagnum moss or peat into the cut so that it is held open, treat the wound with rooting powder, then peg the branch down firmly so that it is buried about 3 inches (8 cm) deep in the compost. I also place a heavy stone on top to make sure that it is held firm. Keep the layer well-watered in dry weather, and in eighteen months it should be rooted. Sever the layer from the parent bush two or three months before lifting it for transplanting elsewhere in the garden.

There are so many hybrids to choose from that the only way to get the right plant is to go along to a nursery when the bushes are in bloom. Check the flower colour and leaf shape, and if possible enquire what the ultimate height will be, then buy the one which fills all requirements.

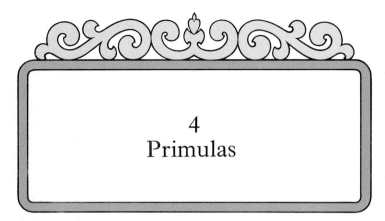

4
Primulas

Primulas are distributed throughout the world. They extend in a band across North America, Europe, including the British Isles, northern India and Asia with the greatest concentration in the latter continent. Some of them, including the well-loved primrose, *Primula vulgaris*, are native to this country. Other natives are *P. veris*, *P. scotica* and *P. farinosa*. There are so many species – well over five hundred – occurring in such widely diverse habitats that Primulas offer a study in themselves. Some grow naturally in moist rock crevices high up in the mountains, whereas others colonise shady forest glades, open meadows, or ribbon the banks of streams with colour. A small percentage of primula species will grow quite happily under ordinary garden conditions. Others need special soils, or the shelter of a frame, or even a heated greenhouse. Such a wide diversity of cultural requirements offers interest to everyone from the novice to the most dedicated of gardeners. Each success acts as a spur to further effort.

There are members of the clan which have been much-loved garden plants for centuries and in consequence have a well-documented history. Our own native primrose, which grows in careless profusion in hedgerows, copses, and woodland from Scotland to the Mediterranean, is particularly well recorded.

Below left: *Primula vulgaris*
Below: *Primula vulgaris* (Double form)

Primula 'Penlan Strain'

Though the type species, the lovely *P. vulgaris*, is by no means easy to establish in the garden, the special garden forms developed from it show no such reluctance. To most people a primrose has yellow flowers, but coloured forms do occur in the wild. *P. vulgaris sibthorpii*, the 'Caucasian primrose', differs in the colour of the petals, which may be purple, red, lilac, white, or, rarely, yellow. The possibility of natural and induced variation is immediately obvious, and gardeners of three hundred years ago were quick to take advantage of this in practical terms. Until quite recently the production and maintenance of double-flowered forms were thought to depend on the plants being frequently lifted, clipped over, and transplanted, so it is surprising that any primrose survived – or gardeners, either. The first variation mentioned is a double cream-coloured flower with a sweet scent, for red or purple variations seem not to have occurred until the Caucasian primrose was distributed in the early 1600s. This blooms earlier than our native primrose, so cross-pollination would need to be contrived, although manipulation would hardly seem necessary as the Caucasian primrose is variable enough without hybridisation. By the mid-seventeenth century in one botanic garden there were growing blue, purple, and white single-flowered forms, but still only the one double-flowered variety. By the eighteenth century double varieties were established, including a double red. Then as now, if reports I have read are accurate, the double white is the easiest to grow, while the best forms of double red are the hardiest, at least in my experience. The source of many double primroses, Ireland, gives a clue to their cultivation in gardens: a sheltered, moist corner suits my plants very well. Varieties generally available are the splendid, four-hundred-year-old 'Double White'; 'Our Pat', amethyst-purple; 'Marie Crousse', violet-red; and 'Bon Accord Gem', rose-coloured. The variety I grew as 'G. F. Wilson' must, I think, be 'Quaker's Bonnet', and extremely difficult, in my experience, to keep alive. Every other year the plants need lifting and dividing, and are then replanted in a new site which has been prepared in advance by digging in, preferably, rotted cow manure, although peat, leaf mould or compost will do.

Primula 'Marie Crousse'

The 'polyanthus', *Primula × variabilis*, is the result of a union between the cowslip, *Primula veris*, and the primrose. Neither of the two parents is easy to establish in gardens, and yet the polyanthus product of the union is one of our most adaptable, tractable, and popular plants – and one of the mysteries of gardening, one of the many mysteries, for this is what captures then holds our interest. Crosses do occur in the wild, and the resulting seedlings are exactly like the oxlip. Indeed, I have found primroses, cowslips, and oxlips all growing together. I have also found cowslips growing alone, or primroses growing alone, but never the oxlip, even though it is considered a distinct species, *P. elatior*. The name 'polyanthus' occurs in seventeenth-century gardening journals, and by the end of the eighteenth century it had become a sought-after florist's flower. These very specialist varieties were, I suspect, the gold- and silver-laced varieties which today have almost disappeared from general commercial cultivation. Now, there are many strains of polyanthus in a wide selection of colours with individual blooms so large that some of the charm and character is being lost. However, many of the old and interesting colour forms still exist and are popular. Names like 'Jack in the Green', 'Jackanapes', and 'Hose in Hose' seem to add to the charm of the plant, and the 'Barnhaven' varieties remain ever popular.

A soil well-supplied with rotted manure or similar humus-forming material will suit polyanthus. The plants should be lifted and divided every second year, or they deteriorate even in the most suitable soil conditions. Alternatively, new stock can be raised from seed each year, for this ensures that you obtain well-flowered plants.

Above left: *Primula elatior*
Above: *Primula veris*

Above: *Primula* 'Hose in Hose'
Above right: *Primula* 'Barnhaven Gold'

The wild species of primula that we call *P. auricula*, of which 'Dusty Miller', is a garden cultivar, is in nature an alpine plant, and this gives a clue to the place which will best suit the species in the garden. They will tolerate a variety of soils if the drainage is good. I dig in a good supply of rotted compost, plus enough crushed stone to provide perfect drainage. As so often happens, hybrids have largely supplanted the species, and the cross between *P. auricula* and *P. hirsuta* was the first recorded,

Primula 'Barnhaven Blues'

resulting in a race of garden auricula collectively known as *P. pubescens*. These are smooth-leaved, and differ quite markedly from the specialist 'Show' and mealy-leaved 'Border' varieties which figure in the Primula Society shows. During the years 1650–1760 it almost became a cult flower, with the highly prized striped and edged show or florist varieties bringing sums in excess of £20 each. The white powder, farina, which dusts the leaves, is soon damaged if the plants are exposed to rain, as is the 'paste' on the centre of the flowers, so this section is cultivated as pot plants, and very handsome they are.

Some of the composts recommended for the proper cultivation of show auricula must have tested the devotion of even the enthusiasts: pigeon or goose dung, blood and similarly noxious materials are offered as essentials.

During the latter half of the nineteenth century came the Asiatic primula, from Sikkim, Nepal, the China–Tibet border – what an Aladdin's cave of plants this area is! Many of the new introductions proved hardier and easier to cultivate than the European species, so were welcomed with greater enthusiasm. The first of these, and still the most popular, is the 'Drumstick Primula', *P. denticulata*, discovered during the 1830s in upper Nepal. Any soil will suit this accommodating plant so long as it is never allowed to dry out. To make certain of the cool, moist root run in which this species delights I dig in compost, peat or well-rotted manure, and my plants flower excellently. Several good

Top: *Primula denticulata* 'Alba'
Above: *Primula denticulata*

colour forms have been selected, ranging from the cool lilac of the species, through to violet, pink, red and pure white. These are best increased by division, but seed is freely supplied and is easy to germinate. Height is 12 to 20 inches (30 to 51 cm) at flowering.

Another Himalayan species worthy of mention is *P. rosea*. A compact little plant, its rose-pink flowers are held 4 inches (10 cm) high, and are a delight in my garden in late April.

Before embarking on a survey of the most garden-worthy Asiatic primula, mention should be made of *P. farinosa* – our native 'Bird's-eye primrose' – which is easily grown in moist, peaty soil. The petal colour varies from light purple to lilac, pink, and a most delicate albino. The flower stems grow 10 inches (25 cm) high with a few or many flowers to a compact head. Seed will germinate two or three weeks after sowing, or old plants which readily form separate crowns may be divided after flowering. The other primula native to these islands is *P. scotica*; found only in the most northerly parts of Scotland, it grows in damp pasture land.

More important from the gardener's viewpoint is the lovely Transcaucasian primrose, *P. juliae*. With the possible exception of the primrose and polyanthus it is the most noteworthy of all the primula, for who can estimate the contribution that hybrids from this species have made to the beauty of our gardens? Among them are 'Wanda', with claret-red flowers, 'E. R. Janes', 'Mauve Queen', and the delectable 'Garryard Guinevere' – the last three from cross-pollination with the common primrose.

Top: *Primula rosea*
Centre: *Primula farinosa*
Above: *Primula juliae*
'Garryard Guinevere'

Primula scotica

First encounters sometimes remain vivid in the memory, and this is certainly true of my discovery of *P. marginata* growing amongst moss-covered stones in the Maritime Alps. Grey-green, deeply toothed leaves dusted with white powder topped by large lavender-blue flowers combined to make this the most beautiful alpine primula. I grow the plants on a ledge in the rock garden where there is full sun and perfect drainage. The hybrids 'Linda Pope' and 'Holden Clough' are also exceptional. Cuttings made of the woody, rhizomatous stems with a tuft of leaves attached and rooted in sandy compost form a simple method of propagation.

Climatic conditions vary a great deal at high altitudes, depending on which part of the earth's surface the measurement is made. At 10 000 feet (3 000 m) in the European Dolomites there is perpetual snow, whereas at 12 000 feet (3 600 m) in the mountains of western China can be found growing rhododendrons, meconopsis, gentians, and primula. So it would follow that a primula growing at that height in China would probably suffer less severe weather than a primula growing at 6 000 or 7 000 feet (1 800 or 2 100 m) in the European Alps, and yet so many of the Asiatic primula do thrive in gardens throughout the British Isles.

Primula marginata

Primula japonica

For twenty years I worked in a garden with wet clay soil in which primulas grew so well that in the stream garden self-sown seedlings had to be hoed off as weeds. Just to show a proper balance, there are Asiatic primulas so temperamental that only the dedicated specialist can succeed in their cultivation.

There is no doubt that the best display of Candelabra primula I have ever seen were growing in moist soil along both banks of a small stream, with light shade but not root competition from oak trees situated on the south side. *P. beesiana* is typical of the section; the rosy-carmine flowers are carried in whorls up stems which are 30 or more inches (76 cm) in height. The arrangement could be described as a series of wheels gradually decreasing in size from bottom to top; the season, June to July. *P. bulleyana* is a better all-round plant, with candelabra spikes of five or more whorls of orange flowers. Both these species flower from mid-June to August.

A moist soil well-supplied with leaf mould, peat, well-rotted manure or compost is eminently suitable. Light overhead shade prevents the flower colour from fading. Primulas will cross-pollinate with others in the same section in a totally uninhibited way to create a multi-coloured race of hybrids, so division is the only method by which colours are kept true to the parent unless the species are kept isolated.

There are several other species in this section which are worth growing where space permits. *P. cockburniana*, a much dwarfer plant at 12 inches (30 cm) high has flowers of an arresting shade of orange, opening slightly earlier than others in the section. In my experience the species is not a good perennial, but cross-pollination between this and other Candelabra species have produced some delightfully vivid coloured hybrids, usually excellent perennials. I just dot groups of *P. cockburniana* at intervals down the border and leave them to cross naturally, which they do with commendable enthusiasm and efficiency.

P. japonica is robust, almost cabbage-like in growth, but for all that it is extremely handsome when in flower. Originating in Japan, it was brought to this country in 1872, and over the years many forms have been developed with purple, red, rose, and white flowers. It varies in height from 18 to 24 inches (46 to 61 cm), depending on soil conditions. 'Miller's Crimson' and 'Postford White' are fine, sturdy varieties. *P. pulverulenta* is another of the section which, though lovely in its own right, has crossed so freely with *P. cockburniana* that the offspring outshine the parents. 'Red Hugh' is particularly fine, with spikes of orange-red candelabra flowers.

Though most gardens have room for only one or two groups of the taller 'Bog' primula, the distinct, strong-growing 'Giant cowslip', *P. florindae*, is worthy of note. I have actually had this plant growing in the stream bed, and it was unharmed by winter floods. This is not a Candelabra primula and is included in the sub-division Sikkimensis. In June to July, when grown in suitably moist soil, it throws up 3-foot (91-cm) high flower stems, topped by heads of forty or more sweetly scented flowers. The hybrid 'Highdown Orange' offers a colour variation on the yellow theme.

Such is the richness and diversity of form contained within the genus that mastery of the problems attendant on growing species from one group by no means assures success in cultivating all primulas. The Petiolares section contains several lovely species to tempt the unwary, none of them in my experience easy to grow, but I have had enough success to encourage me to keep trying. The lovely *Primula bhutanica* is one such plant. The best example I have seen grows in a Himalayan-type climate on the banks of the River Tay in Scotland. With rainfall in excess of 40 inches (1 m) a year and a mild spring the plants really are a delight. The easiest to grow for me is *P. edgeworthii* from the western Himalayas. The yellow-eyed flowers are a delicate pale mauve around an inner white band. They are held posy-like against the nest of white-powdered leaves. Planted in a vertical crevice between peat blocks, *P. edgeworthii* grew very well, flowering in early April. There the crown of leaves was kept dry while the roots explored the permanently wet soil behind. A crevice between stones on the north face of a rock outcrop would do as well. Alternatively, *P. edgeworthii* will flower well when grown in the alpine house. It is interesting that in one Scottish garden I visited the plant grows in a woodland bed where it flowers superbly. Seed offers the best means of increasing stock for me; I have never dared try the root cuttings recommended by those with larger stocks of the plant than I have ever owned.

P. gracilipes, collected in 1846, is widely distributed in northern China and Tibet at elevations of 13 000 to 16 500 feet (4 000 to 5 000 m). It has flowers of bright pink. *P. sonchifolia* has something of the common primrose charm though with azure-

Top: *Primula bhutanica*
Centre: *Primula edgeworthii*
Above: *Primula gracilipes*

Primula sonchifolia

blue, yellow-eyed flowers. Given a shady place in a leaf-mould soil well-supplied with moisture during growth, *P. sonchifolia* is one of the great challenges to the gardener's skill.

Though the Soldanelloides section includes some difficult species, one of the loveliest, *P. nutans*, needs little persuasion to thrive. I sometimes wonder if some of the primulas which have the reputation of being temperamental are not dying of old age, being only short-lived perennials or even monocarpic. Certainly this is the weakness of *P. nutans*, but as seeds germinate quickly and easily, the replacement of casualties is no problem. It was found by that redoubtable plant-hunting priest, Abbé Delavay, in 1884, about 5 000 feet (1 500 m) above sea level growing in pine woods and open, stony pastures. The place which suits my plants well is in the shade border amongst the rhododendrons. There

Primula viali

from mid-June from amongst the hairy leaves rise stalks 1-foot (39-cm) high ending in clustered heads of nodding, bell-shaped flowers, lavender to violet-blue, which are sweetly scented. It is a flower to bring pure delight to anyone who grows it. A peaty or leaf-mould soil is quite suitable.

Though not easy to grow, *P. reidii* is an exquisite member of the same group, growing only 6 inches (15 cm) high. Discovered on the Kumaon, Western Himalayas, in 1884, growing in amongst stones with roots kept permanently moist by melting snow, it needs care in cultivation. Again, I grow my plants with *P. nutans* in peat soil amongst dwarf rhododendrons. I regularly have to replace casualties, but the seven or eight ivory-white or pale-lavender, bell-shaped sweetly scented flowers are reward enough for my trouble. Grown in the alpine house it would present no problem.

In the section Cortusoides, *P. heucheri folia* is a species which will flourish in a humus-rich soil and a shady position. My plants are soundly perennial and grow in the rhododendron border. Until shoots reappeared in April, I thought the first winter had killed them all, because the top growth dies down completely. Loose heads of dark red flowers open on stems 6 inches (15 cm) high during May and June. Seed is set in abundance, or the plants may be divided to increase stock as growth begins in April.

There are some gardeners, and I am one of them, who find it hard to believe that *P. viali* can really belong in the same family as primroses and polyanthus. Once again it was the Abbé Delavay who found the plants growing in moist meadows on Mount Hee-chan-men in Yunnan but, unfortunately, did not collect seed or plants to send home. Then in 1906 George Forrest, the man who introduced so many good garden plants, rediscovered the species. Though supposedly perennial, a considerable percentage of my plants die after flowering, so it is advisable to sow some seed each year. Often growth is slow to begin; in my garden they flower in mid-June. The flowers, remarkably un-primula-like, show colour in June and July. The scape is variable, about 4 inches (10 cm) long, ending in a dense spike of flowers which are crimson in bud opening to bluish-violet. A plant in bloom looks like an outrageously coloured kniphofia ('Red hot poker'). A group of this primula in flower is a sight to remember. They do well in a partially shaded bed, and in soil which is well drained but not liable to dry out. I bury a layer of well-rotted compost or peat 12 inches (30 cm) below the surface before planting to act as a reservoir of moisture, and I get well-flowered *P. viali*.

Several of the primula species have achieved popularity as greenhouse plants. *P. malacoides*, (Fairy primrose), will flower in late winter and early spring from seed sown at intervals from April to June. The peat-based compost is adequate for seed sowing, and germination takes place about three weeks later in a temperature of 65°F. *P. obconica* has larger blooms, and flowers at the same time and with similar treatment. Both should be grown in a cool temperature of 50°F. as, like most of the species, they will not thrive in a hot, dry atmosphere.

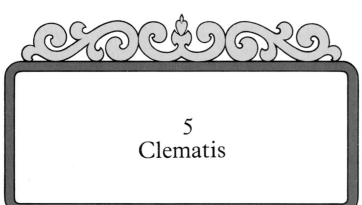

5
Clematis

Clematis and roses are an enduring memory of my childhood years. Though, no doubt, the brush-strokes are bolder, petal colours more vivid in retrospect than they were in reality, both plants still hold a special place in my affections.

There are, in fact, more species of Clematis than of roses, and these are distributed round the temperate regions of the world. The hardy species of gardening interest inhabit China, North America, and Europe. The best-known are the woody climbers, though there are herbaceous forms attractive enough to earn consideration. What surprises me is how little, compared to the rose, clematis figures in poetry, folklore, or garden history. Gerard talks of *Clematis vitalba* as 'Traveller's joy'. The grey-whiskered appearance of the seeds explains, no doubt, the popular name of 'Old man's beard'.

Peculiarly, clematis is included in the buttercup family, which is in itself enough of a contradiction to confuse if a comparison between the two is limited to a visual experience only. The native *C. vitalba*, pleasant enough growing in the hedgerow, is too vigorous for consideration as a garden plant. Not even the fragrance of the double white flowers, reminiscent of almond, compensates for its rampaging persistence.

The European species are of greater merit and importance, particularly the *C. viticella*, which must have been introduced during the sixteenth century, as the blue, red, and double forms are mentioned by writers of the period – first Gerard and then Parkinson – though not with a great deal of enthusiasm for their worth as garden or medicinal plants. *C. viticella* is worthy of note in the historical sense as a parent of some large-flowered garden hybrids. I can remember my father using 'slips' of *C. viticella* as a root-stock on which to graft named varieties that could otherwise be propagated only by means of layers. Gerard also mentioned *C. flammula*, a strong-growing climber up to 10 feet (3 m) high which opens white, sweetly fragrant flowers in late summer. Indeed, it is no surprise that gardeners of an enquiring mind should cross *C. flammula* with *C. viticella* to produce *C.* × 'Rubro marginata', which has reddish-coloured flowers whose only virtue in gardening terms is their fragrance. Possibly, grown over a low wall with sunlight striking through, the flowers may

The author with a beautiful example of *Clematis* 'Jackmanii Superba' outside an Oxfordshire cottage

achieve greater distinction. What I do find very strange is that the lovely *C. alpina* did not reach this country until the late eighteenth century. I first saw the plant in the wild, growing through a 3-foot (0·9-m) high bush of *Rhododendron ferrugineum*. The rose-crimson flower trusses of the 'Alpen Rose' showed the delicate beauty of the blue-petalled clematis to advantage. As the two were growing several thousand feet above sea level on a mountain side, the air of delicacy was an illusion.

C. alpina and the several hybrids which have been raised from it are lovely, robust, easily cultivated garden plants. I have grown the white, semi-double-flowered 'White Moth', the pale blue 'Columbine', and 'Ruby' with rose-red blossoms, all excellent but in no way surpassing the species which grows so readily from seed. The hybrids are increased by means of layers or cuttings of semi-ripened shoots. Only a short while after the establishment of *C. alpina* which, to all intents and purposes, had only to slip across the Channel to reach this country, *C. florida* was introduced from Japan. Although the plant is indigenous to China, the Japanese had the species and several garden hybrids bred from it in cultivation for possibly a hundred years before that. Though the species *C. florida* is not reliably hardy outdoors, as the parent of a race of garden hybrids which flower in advance of the other *C. lanuginosa* they are of prime importance. Clematis can be divided into groups, and *C. florida* gives its name to one which includes species and hybrids flowering in early summer. Gardeners in the less-favoured areas will discover that *C. florida* and its hybrids grow better with wall protection. Of the hybrids 'Belle of Woking' with double, pale mauve flowers, and 'Duchess of Edinburgh' with scented, double white blooms are interesting. In 1912 Mr W. Robinson wrote a monograph devoted to clematis in which he denounces all the double-flowered forms as abominable. The single flowers are so perfectly symmetrical that it seems a pity to change them.

Top: *Clematis alpina* 'Columbine'
Above: *Clematis* 'Belle of Woking'

Top right: *Clematis* 'Barbara Dibley'
Centre right: *Clematis* 'Lasurstern'
Below right: *Clematis* 'Vyvyan Pennell'

Not until 1836 did the second species of importance to the hybridist appear. *C. patens* is thought to be of Chinese origin, but was introduced from Japanese gardens by Philip Franz von Siebold. The wild form has white flowers, yet in all the cultivated forms which I have seen the colour ranges from lilac-grey to violet, so possibly the original von Siebold introduction was also a hybrid. This group comes into flower during May and June. They need some pruning to remove weak or dead wood. I also cut back any shoots that are not required to a strong bud, just to ensure that a crop of young wood is available to replace the old stems which are cut away. Of the hybrids, 'Barbara Dibley' has large flowers of pansy-violet with a deep carmine stripe along each petal. 'Lasurstern' is deep lavender-blue with contrasting white stamens, and it frequently carries a second crop of flowers in early autumn. 'Vyvyan Pennell' has full double blooms of deep violet-blue. Those I grew repeatedly blossomed again in August, but with lavender, single flowers. 'The President' is very popular; the purple sepals have a silvery underside.

The hardiest of the three important Chinese 'parent' species to flower, *C. lanuginosa* was also the last to be discovered by Robert Fortune in China. In nature it grows only 6 feet (2 m) high, though with large flowers. Hybrids are more vigorous, and produce blooms measuring 8 inches (20 cm) or more across from June through to October. Prune out dead and weak growth in February to keep the plants well furnished. Though cross-

hybridising among the various groups has blurred familiar characteristics to some extent, the following qualify as *C. lanuginosa/C. patens* offspring. 'Fairy Queen' has very large, pale flesh-pink-coloured flowers with a deeper central bar, which appear in July and August. 'Nelly Moser', one of the most popular of clematis hybrids, has large mauve-pink flowers, each petal relieved with a carmine-pink central bar. It is a climber which should be grown shaded from direct sun or the colour fades to a washed-out magenta. 'W. E. Gladstone' is of sound constitution, a free-flowering climber, the sepals lavender with deep purple anthers.

There are important species which, though contributing improved forms through seedling selection, are not notable or prolific in cross-breeding. *C. montana*, native of the Himalayas and introduced to this country in 1831, is a superb climber. The flowers appear in such profusion in May as completely to hide branches and whatever support they are trained over. Petal blossoms range in colour from pure white to a beautiful rosy-red and measure 2 to 3 inches (5 to 7 cm) across. Propagation is easily achieved by means of cuttings taken at any month from June to February or by means of seed, which is available in large quantities on a mature plant. This is one of the most effective climbing plants for covering unsightly buildings. I have one specimen of the *C. montana* 'Rubens' with rosy-red flowers growing up through an old apple tree. Also worthy of garden-

Clematis 'Nelly Moser'

Clematis montana 'Rubens'

Clematis montana 'Tetrarose'

Clematis macropetala

space is *C. montana* 'Tetrarose', which has lilac-coloured petals with straw-coloured stamens and attractive bronze foliage.

Many of the species are very beautiful, and the gardener whose sole interest is in the large-flowered hybrids with *C. lanuginosa*, *C. viticella*, *C. patens*, or *C. florida* as parents is not fully exploiting the potential of the genus. *C. armandii* is a useful evergreen climber which, though needing wall protection to grow and flower well, is a very distinctive species. The flowers, which open in April, are pure white, fading to rose as they age. 'Apple Blossom' is a lovely form with the white overlaid on pink.

Though *C. indivisa*, a native of New Zealand, is hardy only in milder areas of the country, I grew it in a cold greenhouse for several years and it is exceptionally beautiful. My plant was the form 'Lobata' and produced enormous crops of pure white flowers in the early spring, even though confined in a 10-inch (25-cm) pot.

What a lot of our best garden plants hail from China! *C. macropetala* is a beautiful species discovered in Kansu early this century. The climbing stems are slender and unobtrusive, while the flowers, from 2 to 4 inches (5 to 10 cm) across, bloom in May. The sepals are violet-blue, and the middle is filled with paler-coloured petal-like segments. It could be described as the Chinese counterpart of the European *C. alpina*, and both are restrained enough in growth to be planted on the steeper slopes of a rock garden. I grow the variety 'Markham's Pink' falling

over a large boulder where the rose-coloured flowers look beautiful against the moss-covered stone. The seed heads, which are covered in feathery tails, are themselves decorative. Seed sown immediately it is fully ripe makes an easy method of increasing stock of the species. Hybrids are best propagated by means of semi-ripe cuttings in June, July, or August.

There are two yellow-flowered species that I have enjoyed growing. The first is *C. orientalis*, which grows wild in northern Asia. Popularly known as the 'Orange-peel clematis', the orange-yellow curved petals are cupped like a partially segmented tangerine. The flowers measure approximately 2 inches (5 cm) across, have a delicate but quite discernible fragrance, and open during August and September. As the buds develop on young growth of the current season, the previous season's shoots can be cut away, as they quite frequently die each autumn anyway. I do all pruning as growth begins in late spring when it is obvious which shoots are, in fact, dead. New stock can easily be raised by sowing seed into general-purpose seed compost in March.

The other yellow-flowered species, *C. tangutica*, is the one I prefer. Although both are very desirable garden plants, *C. tangutica* is of such an easygoing disposition, and flowers so abundantly from July onwards, that it just achieves the higher rating. New plants grow so readily from seed that it costs only effort to stock a large garden. I have used seedlings as ground cover in a limestone rock garden, to grow over shrubs in a mixed border, and had them masking a steep bank in crisp yellow flowers, then later with the silvered seed heads. First introduced from China in 1898 (compared to *C. orientalis*, which appeared in 1730), *C. tangutica* is a comparative newcomer which gained official recognition with an Award of Garden Merit in 1934.

We enjoy the results of creative effort by previous generations of gardeners and hybridists. The first large-flowered species

Above left: *Clematis orientalis*
Above: *Clematis macropetala* 'Snowbird'

Top right: *Clematis* 'Jackmanii Rubra'
Below right: *Clematis integrifolia*

introduced into cultivation flowered only meagrely, so nursery-men started crossing between species to see if hybrid vigour improved the yield of flowers and colour variation.

The first recorded clematis cross was between *C. viticella* and *C. integrifolia*. This occurred at the Pine-apple Nursery belonging to Mr Henderson at St John's Wood in 1835. Henderson's cross is known as *C. × eriostemon* 'Hendersonii'. In 1858 Messrs Jackman of Woking made a double cross using *C. lanuginosa* as the seed parent and the pollen of both *C. × eriostemon* 'Hendersonii' and of *C. viticella* 'Atrorubens'. The famous *C. × Jackmanii* was one of the two resulting seedlings.

So closely were Jackmans associated with clematis that in my early gardening years I thought there was a race of purple flowering plants called not clematis but jackmanii! Certainly the large, violet-coloured, velvet-textured blooms of the Jackmanii are more frequently a feature in gardens than any other species or variety. There seems to be no discernible genetic reason why the yellow-flowered species cannot be crossed with other species and hybrids. Perhaps those who, like myself, have tried in a haphazard way to effect a union between, say, *C. tangutica* and 'Perle

d'Azure', or *C. tangutica* and 'La France' without success, gave up too easily. Possibly in a few years a whole new race of large-flowered, buttercup-yellow-bloomed hybrids will add further contrast to the violets, blues, reds, and whites gracing our gardens.

All clematis I have seen growing wild under natural conditions favoured a habitat amongst shrubs and an alkaline soil. A good basic rule when choosing a place and preparing a soil for clematis would be roots in shade, tops in sun. Lime is not an absolute essential, at least with strong-growing species like *C. montana* or vigorous hybrids. These grew in the very acid soil which I gardened for twenty years, but did not show the robust good health of similar plants established in a magnesium limestone-based loam. Avoid soils which are liable to waterlog or those which become bone dry in the summer. Even on what are termed 'good' soils I still prepare the site for planting. Dig out the existing soil 15 inches (38 cm) deep to leave a hole measuring 2 feet (0·6 m) across. I lose the subsoil in the vegetable garden, then make up the difference by mixing the top soil which is left with compost or horticultural peat, plus a generous dusting of bone meal. This preparation is advisable on average soil, but essential on badly drained clay or light sandy soil. Break up any hard pan at the base of the hole by forking in a shovel full of moist peat or well-rotted compost. The problem of drainage on heavy soils can, to some extent, be overcome by high planting – that is, raising the level by means of paving slabs, bricks, or stone blocks by, say, 10 inches (25 cm) above that of the surrounding soil.

Time of planting depends on the location of the garden, though late April or early May is my preference. By buying plants which are growing in pots the root disturbance is minimal, and with care there is no check to progress at all. Clematis do not like the soil rammed hard around the roots, so I do all the firming down with fingers or only very gently with my boot heel to leave the top of the root ball level with the soil surface. This leaves room for a 4-inch (10-cm) mulch of peat or rotted compost: an

Top left: *Clematis* 'Corona'
Top right: *Clematis* 'Miss Bateman'
Above: *Clematis* 'John Warren'

Top: *Clematis* 'The President'
Above: *Clematis* 'Jackmanii Superba'

excellent way of keeping roots cool and moist. During the first three months after planting out keep the soil well watered, not just round the stem but for 18 inches (46 cm) either side to encourage the roots to spread out and establish. Usually pot-grown plants are tied in to a supporting cane. I leave this in, then just fasten it back to the trellis or whatever the stems are to be trained over. Some years ago I was given a present of the lovely *texensis* hybrid, 'Gravetye Beauty', which has flowers like lapageria. In trying to remove the cane I broke the stem, and the whole plant died. Make sure the stem is held firm, then, as growth starts, train out the young shoots which are very brittle and easily damaged and tie them in position. Each spring after planting I mulch the soil over the roots with well-rotted manure, compost, or peat, and a 4-inch (10-cm) potful of bone meal added to each 2 gallon (9-litre) bucketful of the mulching material. The clematis grown in tubs as patio decoration are given the mulch in spring, then a liquid feed at three-week intervals during the growing season. Another favourite is the lavender-coloured 'Countess of Lovelace'. This has double flowers in the summer and single flowers in the autumn.

Clematis can be used to decorative advantage in various places in the garden. As tub- or container-grown specimens for terrace or patio, they will grow perfectly well in the John Innes No. 3 compost. Suitable varieties to grow in containers would be early flowering, any of the *C. alpina* or *C. macropetala*. The following varieties continue the succession of flowering:

'Corona' – light purple-pink, growing 7 feet (2 m) high;
'Miss Bateman' – white, 6 feet (1·8 m) high;
'The President' – rich purple, 9 feet (2·7 m) high;
'John Warren' – dark pink, 9 feet (2·7 m) high;
'Jackmanii Superba' – dark purple, 9 feet (2·7 m) high.

Clematis 'Countess of Lovelace'

Pruning consists of cleaning out dead and weak growth, except for 'Jackmanii Superba' which should be cut hard back to a good growth bud near soil level.

Each spring carefully remove the top inch or two (2·5 or 5 cm) of soil from the container and top up with more John Innes No. 3 compost. Pruning and careful training in of the young shoots will produce a well-furnished plant, and a spectacular display of flowers. Regular watering and feeding are the other essentials.

For growing through trees or over large walls the stronger-growing species are the best value. Soil preparation is particularly important, as the soil at the base of a tree or foot of a wall is often dry and impoverished.

Among suitable varieties are all forms of *C. montana*. These are excellent and need little pruning. 'Highdown', a variety of *C. vedrariensis*, grows 12 to 18 feet (3·6 to 5·4 m) high, and opens myriads of small pink flowers in May. Again, it needs little pruning. 'Comtesse de Bouchaud', growing 12 to 15 feet (3·6 to 4·5 m) with mauve-pink flowers in August, is decorative but needs hard pruning to maintain vigour. Prune back to a bud just above the base of the previous season's growth. I like to keep all flowering shoots on this variety growing from as near soil level as possible.

When clematis are grown on walls, some sort of supporting trellis or wire will be necessary. Wood or plastic-covered wire is suitable, and is best fixed on wooden battens which provide a clearance from the wall of an inch or so to allow air circulation. Prepare the soil as described, then step the roots out from the base of the wall at least 10 inches (25 cm). No matter how well the soil is made up, that immediately alongside the wall is so dry that the roots struggle to grow. Stepping the roots out solves the problem.

As far as simplifying and summing up the pruning is concerned, most years early-flowering species and varieties – for example, *C. montana* – will need only a general clean-up of dead stems and weak growth. They can be pruned harder if necessary when they grow too large for the space allotted to them. The May-to-June flowering species and varieties, *C. patens*, *C. florida* and *C. lanuginosa* may have the old flowering shoots cut back as the blossoms fade. I also like to thin out over-dense growth and dead or weak branches where necessary in February. Finally, those species which flower on young growths of the current season – Jackmanii is a good example – should be cut right back to within two buds of the old wood. Left unpruned, the plants grow bare at the base, and the flowers open out of sight on the top branches.

There are so many hybrids on offer that I have made no attempt to list them. Which ones to grow must be a personal choice in terms of the site and type of soil available and the flower colour desired. All other considerations aside, clematis are such superb climbing plants that no effort put in to growing them really well will be wasted.

Clematis 'Comtesse de Bouchaud'

6
Irises

Would that all the plants which grace our gardens were named so appropriately! For Iris was one of the Oceanides, goddess of the multi-hued rainbow, and favoured attendant of Juno. Indeed, there could hardly be a more descriptive name, for the iris flowers borrow all the colours of the rainbow. Anyone who doubts this should walk through a garden of modern bearded iris in full bloom. Under the June sunlight the petals of the flowers show innumerable shades and variations of colour.

The Greeks planted iris on the graves of their dead, for just as Mercury conducted the souls of departed males to heaven, so Iris supposedly performed a like service for the women.

The three leaf petals represent valour, wisdom, and faith. Adopted as his device on the Second Crusade by Louis VII of France, iris flowers soon became celebrated as the Fleur de Louis, adapted to Fleur de Luce, and later to Fleur de Lis – the lily flower: not just a change of name but a change of genus when the iris became a lily.

Of the two hundred or more species of iris only two are native to this country: *Iris foetidissima* and *I. pseudacorus. I. foetidissima* is known as 'Stinking Gladwin' or the 'Roast-beef plant'. It is also descriptively referred to as 'Spurge-wort', because substances in the fresh root-stock were much in demand when purging was a popular medicinal cure-all, and is an interesting garden plant.

This species is a slow-growing perennial with purple or pale yellow flowers appearing in early summer. These are followed in due season by a dark brown seed capsule which is full of scarlet-red seeds, much sought after for use in dried flower arrangements. Any reasonably moist and fertile garden soil will suit this species. Propagation is easily effected by means of seed or by division.

I. pseudacorus, (Yellow flag), which grows along the margins of ponds and rivers over much of the British Isles, merits a place in the garden. The yellow flowers, carried on stems 3 feet (0·9 m) high, show up best against a dark background. There are different forms with flower colours which are merely variations on a yellow theme. In one herbal which I read recently the ground-up seeds are suggested as a substitute for coffee. I have

Iris pseudacorus growing on the banks of a Devon marsh

not yet plucked up courage to try the infusion. The form 'Variegata' is a most striking foliage plant: the leaves in spring are striped yellow.

The common iris, *I. germanica*, lays claim to being the oldest plant in cultivation, though I question how this could be proved or disproved. In his discourse on the medicinal properties of plants, Pliny describes with great exactitude how the roots which contain these properties should be dug up. *I. germanica* is a strong-growing species which shows extensive variations in form and flower colour. The most notable form is *florentina*, cultivated since the times of ancient Greece. This is the source of orris, which is made from the violet-scented, powdered rootstock used for hundreds of years in the perfumery trade. Nowadays, *I. pallida* has largely replaced it for this purpose. *I. germanica florentina* is still grown in commercial quantities in Italy, Egypt, Iran, and India. For toiletry preparations the roots need to be well dried before the violet scent is apparent.

Before becoming involved in the description of the best species of iris available for cultivation in the garden, let us consider first the characteristics of the iris. There are two distinct types of root systems. One grows from bulbs or bulb-like corms and contains some very lovely spring-flowering species. The other group has a stout stem-like root – rhizomatous or fibrous. Fortunately, most of the species are hardy outdoors in this country, and by careful selection the garden can provide iris in flower for eight or nine months of the year. In one respect they are easily recognisable: that is by the shape of the flowers, which throughout the species are remarkably similar, with three outer, reflexed petals, often bearded, and three inner, smaller, upright petals known as standards.

Though iris are divided for the convenience of the botanically minded into eleven groups, for my purpose they are better considered in terms of flowering times. The season begins with *I. unguicularis*, whose flowering period in favoured areas can, by judicious selection of varieties, be extended from November to early spring. As would be expected of a plant whose natural home is the eastern Mediterranean, *I. unguicularis* (syn. *I. stylosa*) needs a well-drained soil and the sunniest position which the garden affords. In my last garden a bed made up under the overhanging eaves of the house on a south-facing wall proved excellent. To make certain that the drainage was correct I mixed in a generous dressing of sharp sand until the soil must have been poor to the point of sterility. In this arid medium, encouraged by an annual dressing of leaf mould mixed with dried seaweed fertiliser, the iris produced a succession of flowers which made even grey February tolerable. Recently a friend introduced me to a variety called 'Walter Butt' which carried blooms of palest lilac, in my opinion inferior to the type. A feature of species and hybrids is the delicate fragrance of the flowers – like sun-warmed violets. All grow to about 20 inches (51 cm) tall.

Of the bulbous species which can be persuaded into flower in late winter and early spring, I have only appreciative praise. In

Below left: *Iris unguicularis*
Below: *Iris danfordiae*

Iris winogradowii

most gardens there is a sheltered corner which gathers every ray of sunshine as a miser hoards gold; this is the place to select for *I. histrioides*. The flowers, which appear before the leaves, are large, vivid blue, the fall petal traced with an orange-crested beard. Frequently I have had this species flowering through a carpet of snow with unblemished petals.

I. danfordiae is a yellow-petalled counterpart to the blue *I. histrioides*, and is not so reliably perennial. The bulbs flower well the first year after planting, then divide into a multitude of bulblets none large enough to produce more than leaves in subsequent seasons. They are so lovely that I consider money spent on new stock each year a good investment.

The best-known species, available in several different colour forms, is the delectable, sweet-scented *I. reticulata*. In the type species which I grow the petals are deep violet-blue. There are so many varieties, including hybrids with *I. histrioides* that it is almost a case of being spoiled for choice. 'J. S. Dijt', red-purple, 'Cantab', light blue, and 'Harmony', sky-blue, are a choice selection. Also a particular favourite of mine is the species with lemon-yellow flowers, *I. winogradowii*, which grows wild in the Caucasus.

Iris reticulata

Given a well-drained soil with a top dressing of seaweed fertiliser, bone meal, or meat, fish and bone meal, both *I. histrioides* and *I. reticulata* maintain good flowering colonies. All the bulbous, spring-blooming irises described grow 4- to 6-inch (10- to 15-cm) high flowering stems, but leaf growth extends to 12 inches (30 cm) or more. Plant the bulbs 3 to 4 inches (8 to 10 cm) deep during autumn.

There is another group of spring-flowering, so-called 'bulbous-rooted' irises which need special cultivation – the Juno. All species in the group require good drainage and a hot, sun-baked position. In northern gardens they are best accommodated in a raised frame filled with a sandy compost. During very cold weather the frame can be kept closed, and again in summer when the bulbs are ripening the glass will protect the plants from

Iris bucharica

excess rain. The easiest to grow of this group, *I. bucharica* has a 12-inch (30 cm) high leaf fan. Curiously shaped yellow and white flowers open during early spring. *I. albo-marginata* has attractive grey-blue flowers. The bulbs are planted in September 4 inches (10 cm) deep in a well-drained soil.

Flowering later in spring, usually early to mid-May, *I. douglasiana* and *I. innominata* of the Apogon group represent an entire change in character. Their leaves are evergreen, growing from root-like underground stems. Flowers on 12-inch (30-cm) stems vary in colour from pink, lilac, yellow to white, with the petal veins in contrasting shades of the base tint. Any good garden soil which does not either become waterlogged in winter

Below left: Juno species growing at the Royal Botanic Garden, Kew
Below: *Iris albo-marginata*

Tall bearded irises in full bloom
in a Nottinghamshire garden

or dry out completely in summer will grow both species success-
fully. Increase by seed or division is easily achieved.

The bearded iris is the most easily recognisable and familiar
of all the clan. Indeed, it is of some consolation to anyone who
tries to unravel the very complex iris lineage that in all parts –
root, leaf, and flower – they are so distinctive. The first specialist
hybridiser of bearded, flag or German iris was a Frenchman,
Lémon, who began selective cross-pollination using several
species in the early 1800s. *I. germanica* is not, as I assumed,
responsible for the immense range of tall, intermediate and
dwarf May- and June-flowering bearded forms listed by nurserymen at present. The real ancestors are *I. variegata, I. pallida,
I. trojana,* and, more recently, *I. chamaeiris,* which has been used
to produce smaller, more manageable varieties.

When comparing the small-flowered, rather funereal-
coloured blues and purples of earlier varieties (the main virtue of
which was the ability to survive in any soil or situation) with the
rainbow-hued hybrids of today, the transformation is barely
credible. Whenever the hybridist embarks on an expanding
breeding programme with ever-larger, more extravagantly
coloured flowers as the sole purpose, inevitably, other less
advantageous characteristics appear. Modern hybrids are not so
hardy, nor do they adapt so readily to a wide range of soils or
situations. Flowers are enormous and multi-hued, the petals
crimped and ruffled, but they are carried on tall stems which are
easily damaged by strong winds or heavy rain.

The dwarf iris, from crosses between the tall sorts and *I.
chamaeiris,* are better value for the small garden. There still
remains the challenge of breeding to achieve a race of bearded iris

with the hardiness of 'Kochii' and the petal colours of 'Mulberry Rose'. Those wishing to grow a selection of modern varieties will need to choose from the hundreds available, as new ones are being introduced each year. Fortunately, the early hybrids from *I. pallida* × *variegata* are preserved to enjoy a new popularity as labour-saving garden plants.

Bearded iris are plants of the sunshine, and will not flower unless they are fully exposed in a south-facing border. A well-drained soil is another essential, preferably alkaline in reaction. In my last garden I had of necessity to grow several hundred new varieties of bearded iris in a heavy, lime-free, clay soil. Working in heavy dressings of limestone chippings improved drainage and the lime content enough to make conditions acceptable to the iris, which grew and flowered well.

The time of planting is important, and should be carried out just before the new roots develop. One of the characteristics of the bearded iris is that after flowering a whole new root system starts growing, so lifting, dividing, and replanting should be done as the last flower dies in early July. Choose young, vigorous, disease-free roots (rhizomes), each with a good fan of leaves. Before planting I shorten the leaf growth by half to prevent them being blown about by the wind. Adjust the depth of planting so the root (rhizome) is left exposed on the surface. Once planting is completed I dust the soil around the root with basic slag or superphosphate, which seems to encourage strong root growth. Dividing and replanting can be carried out at three- or four-year intervals, as the roots get overgrown and flower only sparsely. A dusting of fertiliser containing superphosphate and potash each year in April is all the supplementary feeding that this group of iris requires.

The Apogon group, which includes the spring-flowering American species iris, *I. douglasiana* and *I. innominata* previously described, also harbours notable summer-flowering species. One of the easiest to accommodate, requiring soil which does not dry out in summer, is *I. sibirica*, native of Europe and Asia, and certainly cultivated in this country before the seventeenth century. This is a splendid garden plant which, once installed, asks only to be left undisturbed. The grass-like foliage is a foil to broad-leaved hosta or primula. My choice of varieties carry flowers on stems protruding well above the foliage: 'Dreaming Spire', a dark blue; 'Sea Shadows', a fine mid-blue; and 'Anniversary', white.

One of the inexplicable complications of iris classification is the way in which easily grown species share the same group as those which are rare and difficult to grow. Included in the Laevigatae group with the easygoing American and European species are two lovely Japanese species brought to this country midway through the last century. First to arrive was *I. kaempferi*, which in the quality of its velvet-textured flowers rivals the orchid. In order to discover the best conditions for growing this rather temperamental beauty I tried planting one in shallow water, another in moist soil at the pool edge, and a third in a specially prepared moisture-retentive bed. I removed the soil,

Iris 'Curlew' (Intermediate bearded)

Below: *Iris* 'One Desire' (Tall bearded)
Top right: *Iris sibirica* 'Sea Shadows'
Below right: *Iris sibirica* 'Anniversary'

which was lime-free, to a depth of 18 inches (46 cm), spread a thick layer of well-rotted manure in the hole, then replaced the soil, mixing in more rotted manure at the same time. The planting (from containers) was carried out in mid-May. Pool-edge planting needs no special soil preparation, but those grown in shallow water are best grown in the open-work plastic baskets specially designed to keep the crown dry. The varieties 'Rose Queen', 'Purple Splendour' and those listed under 'Higo' hybrids are amongst the loveliest flowers which ever graced our gardens. They grow to around 30 inches (76 cm) in a lime-free soil.

The other Japanese introduction, *I. laevigata*, will grow well if planted beside a garden pool or stream. In one garden I know the lavender-blue and white-flowered hybrids luxuriate in a bed of peaty soil, kept well-watered during very dry weather. The leaves of this species are broader paler green than those of *I. kaempferi*, particularly those of the pastel-shaded flowered forms. The species introduced from Japan in 1856 has broad-

petalled, clear blue flowers. In the form *I. albo-purpurea* the blue is mottled and suffused with white, which, though very attractive, is less pleasing to me than the pure white 'Alba'. Some of the best examples of *I. laevigata* hybrids are to be found in the Bagatelle garden in Paris. The less common *I. laevigata* 'Variegata' has the bonus of attractive foliage to complement the violet-blue flowers. Though closely enough related to *I. kaempferi* for crosses to have been made between the species, neither *I. laevigata* nor the hybrids seem to scorn a soil which contains lime.

The species *I. ochroleuca* (the Butterfly iris) is a worthy garden plant. The leaves are over 3 feet (0·9 m) long, and a succession of cream white flowers are borne in late June.

Why *I. xiphioides* enjoys the popular name of 'English iris' when it hails from the Pyrenees is one of those unexplained garden mysteries. Merchants trading from Bristol imported the bulbs, which established themselves so readily that they became a common garden feature. Eventually the bulbs were exported back to Holland. Could this possibly explain the popular name

Above and left: *Iris laevigata* 'Alba'

Below left: *Iris laevigata* 'Variegata'
Below: *Iris ochroleuca*

Above: *Iris laevigata* 'Apaisie'
Above right: *Iris laevigata* 'Tamura'

Iris xiphium 'Yellow Queen'

English iris? Soil prepared by trenching and manuring seems to suit this iris. For six years I planted the bulbs 4 inches (10 cm) deep along a trench that in the previous years had grown sweet peas, and they flowered exceedingly well. The type colour is blue, though mixed varieties give the best display.

Useful also as a cut flower *I. xiphium*, 'Spanish iris', is closely related to English iris, though flowering slightly earlier. They are available in a wide range of colours, and grow in well-drained soil and full sun. Their height is between 18 and 24 inches (46 and 61 cm). The 'Dutch iris' (a hybrid between *I. xiphium* and *I. tingitana*) is reported as being a selected form of the Spanish iris. These flower early, and include amongst the blue and violet some fine yellow-flowered varieties – for example, 'Yellow Queen'.

I. tingitana, a native of Morocco, is the first to flower. The popular 'Wedgwood', so excellent for forcing, is reputed to be a variety of this species – which surprises me, for I have always bought it as Dutch iris.

Next into bloom come the Dutch *I. xiphium* hybrids such as 'Yellow Queen' and 'Excelsior', followed by the lovely *I. filifolia*, then the Spanish and British 'Celestial', 'Sweet Scented', 'King of the Blues', and 'Leviathan'.

The earliest varieties are potted up in August, then watered and stood outside in a cool place until moved under glass in early October. In a temperature of 50°F. flowers are ready for cutting in late November. The main crop bulbs are potted up in September and stored in a cool place until they are moved inside in late November. They are kept at a temperature of 48°F. until the flower buds show, rising to 55°F., and cutting can usually commence in February. Further stocks are moved in to keep up a succession throughout the winter. The main requirement for success is to keep the bulbs well-supplied with moisture without letting the soil become stagnant.

The range and variety of iris is immense, some being tiny enough to grow in company with the smallest rock plants. Certainly, I would miss those which grow and flower in my own garden.

7
Dahlias

The cultivated forms of dahlia show remarkable variability in flower shape and colour. Indeed, anyone who has grown dahlias in any quantity for several years will have discovered how a variety can produce, without any visible stimulus, a flower or flowers of entirely different colour. The change is usually, but not invariably, in colour only; the shape remains that of the parent variety. Even bearing this instability in mind, it comes as a surprise to those gardeners who consider the art and craft of gardening to have their origins in the British Isles to learn that when the dahlia was discovered four hundred years ago in Mexico by Spanish invaders, it was already being grown by the Aztecs.

One way in which to appreciate how dramatic and far-reaching are the changes which have been made by hybridisation is to compare a lovely wild species like *Dahlia merckii* with one of the large, flamboyant entries in the Giant-flowered Class at any dahlia show. They are in truth four hundred years apart.

The first dahlias were introduced to Europe in 1789 when the Botanic Gardens in Mexico sent seeds to the Royal Gardens in Madrid. One of the seedlings flowered in the following year, and the genus was named *Dahlia* in honour of the Swedish botanist Dahl. Such are the vagaries, the happy chances on which immortality is built. The Aztecs who grew dahlias take second place to a Swedish botanist whose only claim to honour was that he studied under Linnaeus. But for the dahlia, no doubt, Dr Dahl would long ago have been forgotten.

At first, encouraged by the plant's forming potato-like tubers, hopes were kindled that the dahlia would prove to be a new vegetable. Having tasted roast dahlia tubers, I would agree that though non-poisonous they are certainly disagreeably unappetising.

Modern students have identified the first species introduced as *D. pinnata, D. coccinea* and *D. rosea*. Though these early species were not of spectacular floral merit, even the first seedlings to flower showed the family instability when some of them developed semi-double flowers. Possibly seed from what were purported to be species were, in fact, hybrids arising from crosses made between the species.

Hybrid dahlias being taken
to a Mexican market

A collection of seeds sent directly from Mexico to Europe in
1804 produced a very variable crop of seedlings with single and
semi-double flowers. The first fully double blooms were bred by
M. Donkelaar in 1812. By 1814 botanists working in the Botanic
Garden at Louvain had produced the first white dahlia, several
large-flowered doubles and dwarf plants, which were to give rise
to those most popular dahlias, the versatile 'Coltness hybrids'. In
the period between 1814 and 1828 stock of the new races of
dahlias were imported to Britain from Europe, and the gardeners
of that era quickly recognised the potential of the flower which
provides colour in the garden until October.

Unlike the rose, rhododendron, and many popular flowers
which take several years to reach flowering size, dahlias can be
grown from seed to maturity in one growing season. Even
considering the speed with which new generations of hybrid
dahlia can be produced, it is incredible just how many varieties
were being offered in catalogues by 1820: doubles, semi-doubles,
singles, and the first bicolours in almost the comprehensive range
of colours that gardeners expect of present-day nurseries. The
dahlia had, indeed, become, according to London's *Ency-*
clopaedia of Gardening, 'the most fashionable flower' in these

Above left: *Dahlia* 'Corina'
(Single-flowered)
Above: *Dahlia* 'Omo'
(Single-flowered)

islands. Though the first three-quarters of the nineteenth century showed a progressive development in the shape and quality of the flowers, it was along broadly established lines. For example, the earliest Pompon dahlias were ill proportioned, the small flower perched on the end of a 3- to 4-foot (0·9 to 1·2 m) stem. Selective breeding reduced the stem length to correspond proportionately with the size of the flower. Varieties increased to the extent that in 1841 Harrison's Nursery listed over a thousand double-flowered varieties, presumably of the form which subsequently would be classified as formal Decorative dahlias.

The next development in the hybridising field came when a Mr Van der Burgh took delivery of a parcel of plants from Mexico. Nearly all had died *en route*, but fortunately one, a dahlia tuber, had survived. This was planted and grew to produce a scarlet flower with long-quilled petals. Subsequently this variation, named *D. juarezii*, was cross-pollinated with existing varieties to produce a new class – the Cactus dahlia. When a new species of distinctly different form is imported, a great impetus is given to the propagation of hybrids, and this was the result once the quilled, petalled *D. juarezii* presented itself.

Cactus dahlias crossed with show or Decorative dahlias generated sufficient variation to warrant the addition of several new classes to the list, including the Paeony-flowered, which is a direct result of the cross between Cactus and the ball-type show dahlia.

Dahlias are classified for show purposes according to flower shape: 'Single-flowered', with a single outer ring of petals around an open central disc; 'Anemone-flowered', which have the ring or rings of flattened petals surrounding a central boss of shorter, tubular petals – rather like a quilled pincushion; 'Collerette', with the ring of outer petals complemented by a ring of shorter, inner petals often of a contrasting colour; 'Paeony-flowered' – less fashionable now – with a looser, less regular petal formation, precisely resembling the border Paeonia. 'Decorative' dahlias are full double with flat or slightly incurving petals in a perfectly globular head. 'Ball' dahlias are full double

Dahlia 'Opal' (Ball)

Above: *Dahlia* 'Fascination'
(Paeony-flowered)
Above right: *Dahlia* 'La Cierva'
(Collerette)
Right: *Dahlia* 'Kidd's Climax'
(Giant Decorative)

Below: *Dahlia* 'Honey'
(Anemone-flowered)
Below right: *Dahlia* 'Winston Churchill'
(Miniature Decorative)

Above: *Dahlia* 'Salmon Symbol'
(Medium Semi-Cactus)
Left: *Dahlia* 'Doris Day'
(Small-flowered Cactus)

Below: *Dahlia pinnata*

varieties. No one can predict precisely what sort of flowers the seedlings will eventually produce. They will all flower, and amongst the very average blooms there may be one or more of such outstanding merit that it achieves a name and distinction on the show bench.

Bedding dahlias are more predictable, and many thousands of 'Coltness' and similar dwarf varieties are raised annually for use in summer bedding schemes. Seed should be sown under glass at any time from February to April, depending on how well the greenhouse is heated. For April sowings usually no supplementary heat is needed – except in very cold, freak conditions such as those experienced in late April 1981. Sow the seed into a standard peat or loam compost in the usual way, then cover the trays with newspaper to conserve heat and moisture. Once the seedlings are big enough to handle they can be pricked off and grown on in exactly the same way as for cuttings.

A bed of dahlias in full bloom in September sunlight is a pleasing sight. Like any other garden plant they will flower all the better in well-prepared soil. Choose a warm, sheltered site in full sun: as one would expect with plants from Mexico they appreciate warmth and dislike cold winds. In order to make certain that the soil is in good condition I dig in heavy dressings of rotted manure or similar organic matter at some time during the winter. Then, ten days before planting I lightly fork in 2 oz per square yard (57 g per 0·8 square m) of a complete fertiliser just to give the young dahlia a proper start. How far apart the plants are spaced depends on the variety: about 18 inches (46 cm) each way for bedding types, an average of 24 inches (61 cm) for the rest – except the giant varieties which in the course of a single season grow 4 or 5 feet (1·2 or 1·5 m) by as much across. Water each plant in, then make sure that each stem is tied securely to a support. Keep them well supplied with feed and moisture to build up a strong flowering framework. To encourage the development of side shoots, pinch out the growing point in July, otherwise this produces a premature flower which inhibits the growth of the side shoots that will carry the main display in late August.

In order to achieve show quality blooms, stopping, shoot thinning, and disbudding will be necessary; in this way all the plant's energies are concentrated into the production of a limited number of potentially perfect flowers.

After the frosts of autumn have blackened the dahlia foliage, all top growth is cut away and the tubers are lifted. Leave the roots in an airy shed to dry, a process which makes it easy to clean away all the soil which adhered to the roots when they were lifted. With an old pair of scissors I clip off the whisker-like roots which grow on the swollen tubers. The dahlia stems have a pithy central core, and to reduce the risk of this holding moisture to cause rotting, I push a piece of heavy-gauge wire through the middle of the stem. This clears out the pith to leave an air passage which thoroughly dries out the central root portion. In order to prevent a mix-up in the spring I tie a label to the stem with the name of the variety clearly printed on it.

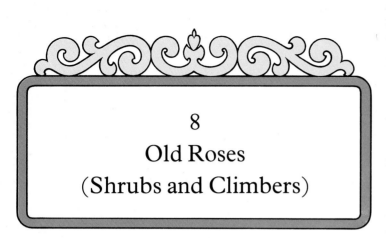

8
Old Roses
(Shrubs and Climbers)

The rose is the most celebrated of all garden flowers. In one form or another, and for a variety of purposes roses have been cultivated for at least three thousand years. Throughout every period of recorded history there are references to roses. In festival and legend roses have figured as a token of passion, esteem, fidelity, triumph, and, on occasion, remembrance.

Like the stages of man, the rose has played in its time many parts. Roman brides and bridegrooms were crowned with wreaths of roses and verbena plucked by the bride herself, typifying love and purity. In more martial vein Persian warriors wore garlands of roses on their shields. The Persians believed also that the roses burst into bloom only when the nightingale sang. Rose petals were scattered in the path of conquering armies, and were used as decoration on the figureheads of warships. A wreath of roses worn around the head was in the more degenerate days of the Roman empire supposed to prevent intoxication. Yet the flower also figured frequently in burial ceremonies, particularly those of the Greeks and Romans, who decorated their tombs, as the inscription at Ravenna indicates, with 'The Queen of Flowers'.

Roses also played an important part in the pharmacopoeia as a constituent of herbal medicine, to strengthen the heart, stomach, and liver, to stop coughs, to prevent vomiting, and to cure lung diseases. A cosmetic in rose water, skin creams, and lotions, the flower has for centuries been used for skin care.

The rose has been studied by botanists, extolled by poets, cultivated and hybridised by gardeners. It has been an object of veneration, decoration, and utility, an associate of mirth and celebration, a companion of death and lamentation.

There are many fascinating fables accounting for the various colours of roses. Venus, trying to hide Adonis from the vengeance of Mars in a thicket of roses, pricked herself on a thorn, staining the white rose-red with her blood. Ayeshah, wife of Mohammed, suspected of infidelity with a Persian youth, was asked to dip a bunch of white roses in the fountain to prove her innocence. Should the flowers emerge unchanged, the accusation would be seen as a lie. They were plunged into the water where they turned yellow – which is, indeed, fortunate, for the same

Climbing roses at the
Bagatelle in Paris

rose is the parent of so many of our yellow bedding roses. Fact, legend, folklore are so inextricably intertwined that even research historians have not untangled the web sufficiently to reveal the whole story. The argument over which are the true species and which natural hybrids flares up at intervals.

Some facts do emerge. The birthplace of the rose as we know it was discovered to be Persia, but fossilised roses have been discovered in Europe, America, and Asia. The 'foundation' roses, well-known and widely grown throughout Europe in the sixteenth century, were *Rosa gallica*, *R. moschata*, *R. damascena*, and *R. alba*. These are generally supposed to have come from 'the land of the Saracens' – that is, the region of Arabic–Mohammedan influence in Syria and areas nearby. Persia's contribution to rose history came in the introduction of *R. foetida*

in the late nineteenth century, which brought a true yellow to European roses for the first time. However, the birthplace of the modern rose is surely China, as it was these introductions that brought in repeat flowering, or the remontant habit, so important in modern roses.

The profitable cultivation of roses as a commercial venture began in Persia about the year 1612 with the distillation of attar of roses, an industry which spread into Europe through Turkey. The largest centre of rose growing for perfumery was located in the valley of Struma in the Balkans where Damask roses were grown in large quantities to provide the material for processing. Even three hundred years ago growing roses for garden ornament was not widespread. There were possibly a few plants in monastery gardens, or in the large demesne. Not until the Empress Joséphine began to collect roses for her garden at Malmaison, France, early last century, in all over a hundred species and varieties, did rose growing become fashionable. Since then interest in roses, their cultivation and the breeding of new varieties has increased at a still accelerating speed. Specialist

Climbing roses floodlit at
La Roseraie de l'Haÿ les Roses, Paris

Rosa canina

societies were soon formed to cater for those who shared an enthusiasm for growing roses even more precise in formation and exquisite in colour.

The story of the rose in Britain is well documented. In 1629 Parkinson writes of 'a great variete of roses' which grew in his garden. Not counting the species, those amounted to only thirty sorts. I wonder what effect a modern list of roses would have on that learned gentleman!

In this country there are a number of wild species. The sap from the roots of *R. canina* is listed in herbals as a cure for rabies, which explains the popular name Dog rose and the botanical title. The Field rose, *R. arvensis*, smaller than the Dog rose, is quite common in southern and central England. The Burnet rose, *R. pimpinellifolia*, with creamy-white flowers and prickly stems, is found in coastal areas. Sweet briar, *R. eglanteria* or *R. rubiginosa*, is the least common, growing mainly on lime soils, and is distinguished by dark pink petals and more rounded leaflets which are sweetly fragrant. *R. villosa*, the Downy rose, is identified by double-toothed leaflets, pink flowers, and very large fruits which are distinctly ornamental, useful also for making preserves. The flowering times are more or less the same in all the native species, though there is not sufficient difference in growth or character of flower for cross-pollination to produce any wide variation in the resulting hybrids. *R. canina* has, however, been used extensively as a root-stock on which to bud Shrub, Hybrid tea, and Floribunda roses, as it will grow well in most soils, an adaptability which is of considerable importance.

In their wild state roses occur only in the northern hemisphere, and of the two hundred or so species only about one-tenth figure in the parentage of popular modern hybrids. Again, Gerard in his *Herbal* written in 1597 lists amongst others five roses which have made an important contribution: *R. gallica, R. damascena, R. centifolia, R. alba* and *R. moschata*.

Below: *Rosa eglanteria*
Below right: *Rosa centifolia* 'Cristata'

Left: *Rosa damascena*

Below: *Rosa* 'Céleste'

Far left: *Rosa gallica officinalis*
Left: *Rosa gallica versicolor*
Right: *Rosa moschata*

R. gallica, the French rose, being among the most ancient, is considered to be one of the earliest which produced semi-double and double flowers; these vary in colour from pink to dark red. The dwarf, compact habit and healthy, dark green foliage would undoubtedly be noted by early rosarians as desirable qualities in a garden plant. *R. gallica* is one parent of the hybrid China and Bourbon roses. It is the only true red-flowered species native to Europe. The red semi-double Apothecary's rose, *R. gallica officinalis*, is unusual in that the colour and scent of the flower is retained almost totally in the dried state. They were at one time widely used as a tonic tisane.

R. damascena, the Damask rose, forms a prickly bush up to 5 feet (1·5 m) high with white to red, very fragrant flowers opening in June and July. Apart from giving rise to the much-discussed 'York and Lancaster' rose, it is also one parent of the Hybrid Perpetuals which became popular in the nineteenth century.

R. centifolia, the Provence rose, is a fairly loose-habited shrub growing to 4 feet (1·2 m) or slightly more. The clear pink flowers appear late in June or July, and are frequently featured in Dutch flower paintings of the nineteenth century.

The White rose of York, *Rosa × alba semi-plena*, must be one of the earliest known hybrids, possibly between *R. dumetorum* and *R. gallica*. It is a spreading shrub up to 8 feet (2·4 m) high, with white flowers quite often shaded with pink, and grey-green leaves. One of the loveliest hybrids from *R. × alba*, which appeared in the late eighteenth century, is 'Céleste', a perfectly delightful shrub. The soft pink flowers against the grey-green leaves combine to present a picture which will grace any garden.

R. moschata is a vigorous, rampant climber, which I have seen growing 30 feet (9 m) along a retaining wall and, in the same garden, at least the same distance through and over an old tree. More than four hundred years have elapsed since it was introduced to gardeners in Britain from Italian gardens. The flowers, which open in August continuing until the frosts, are single white and intensely fragrant. The true *R. moschata* of garden

tradition is rare possibly because it is tender and needs a sheltered corner. Also, the late flowering habit would not now be considered an advantage when ever-blooming climbers are available which flower five months of the year and take up less space. Nevertheless, *R. moschata* could at least lay claim to being the first climbing rose to be grown in British gardens, and even more important, through the China roses is an ancestor of the modern HT, the Hybrid Musk, and some of the popular ramblers. Indeed, it is surprising just how many modern roses originate in the distant past from one of the five roses listed by Gerard.

Fresh impetus and interest was injected into rose hybridisation and growing by the introductions from China of roses which were repeat, or, as they are termed, 'perpetual blooming', a character not evident in the species cultivated in this country or Europe. There were four original China roses introduced to European gardens about 1790, but two – 'Slater's Crimson', and, more important, 'Parson's Pink' because it was hardier – arrived first to be adopted very quickly by nurserymen. 'Parson's Pink' crossed with the already established musk roses produced the Noisette roses, which are repeat flowering. They are best pruned during the winter, when weak shoots and worn-out branches should be taken out.

'Gloire de Dijon' was one of the early Noisette with well-formed flowers, buff-yellow tinted pink, in evidence from June to September. This hybrid flowers with reasonable freedom when grown on a north wall, and is still a widely acclaimed variety.

'Aimée Vibert' is even older, with white flowers which look best if the 15-foot (4·5-m) shoots are allowed to arch out naturally on a bank or over a retaining wall.

The marriage between the China roses and Damask produced the Bourbon group, which originate from the Ile de Bourbon. It is a mixed group characterised by vigorous growth, rather lax habit, and globular blooms. Most splendid of these is

Top left: *Rosa* 'Gloire de Dijon'
Top right: *Rosa* 'Parson's Pink'
Above: *Rosa* 'Mme Isaac Pereire'

Opposite
Top: *Rosa moyesii*
Centre: *Rosa xanthina* 'Canary Bird'
Below: *Rosa* 'Frau Karl Druschki'

the 'Zéphirine Drouhin' which, though introduced in 1868, still retains a unique place in gardens. The stems are thornless, the young foliage copper, flushed purple. Vivid cerise-pink flowers, delightfully scented, open in continuous succession from June to Christmas given freedom from frost. 'Zéphirine Drouhin' alone assures the Bourbon rose of a proud place in the record books. Another of the truly worthwhile Bourbon hybrids is 'Mme Isaac Pereire', which grows into a large bush. The flowers are large and cup-shaped; the deep pink petals, rolled at the tips, are very fragrant.

Almost as the first crosses using the Chinese introductions were being made came two more roses from China. The first was bought from a Cantonese nursery – 'Hume's Blush', described as a Tea-scented China. The second, 'Park's Yellow Tea-scented China', also Cantonese, arrived a few years later. For the rose breeder it added a new colour to be used in cross-pollination. The fragrance was unlike that of the established varieties. 'Used' is possibly the wrong word to describe early attempts at cross-pollination. Growers left things very much to nature, planting groups of selected bushes near to each other for the bees to work on. Only in the late 1800s did the hybridiser start selective pollination by hand, a process which enabled exact details of parentage to be kept.

Once begun, new species of roses were continually being introduced and entered for use into the rose breeders' stud books. Two are individual and exceptional garden plants. _R. moyesii_ commemorates the Reverend Moyes. Introduced in 1903, the tall, upright bush with fern-like foliage and single flowers of dusky crimson is a noble sight. In autumn, when large flask-shaped hips show vivid red against the yellowing leaves, the bush is once more superb. I have grown several dozen _R. moyesii_ from seed over the years; all have been good, although several were outstanding, with large, dusky-red blooms the colour of bonfire embers on a frosty night. The other, from Korea, is _R. xanthina_, of which the form 'Canary Bird' is the best known. The canary-yellow flowers which cover the long arching branches in May to June are borne in such profusion that the bush becomes a fountain of gold.

The influence of the Chinese roses was given fresh impetus when the rather tender, yellow-flowered climber, _R. gigantea_, was discovered and the possibility realised of raising climbing roses with yellow flowers. So the raising of more new garden roses progressed from the casual, open pollination of pre-1870 to the hand-selected, and finally to the line-breeding, tissue culture of the present day.

Certain roses grow best on a particular type of soil. Burnet roses, as would be expected, succeed on a light soil. Most of these will grow in well-maintained garden soil and a place in the sun.

Hybrid Perpetuals are a mixture of so many groups, starting with Bourbon roses, that tracing the family tree is extremely difficult. Best-known of the Hybrid Perpetuals is 'Frau Karl Druschki', the loveliest of white roses but unfortunately without scent. Growth is vigorous, up to 5 feet (1·5 m) with well-formed

white flowers opening in succession over many months. 'Hugh Dickson', another HP, was for a long time the best red rose for growing on a wall or fence. The height is around 9 feet (2·7 m), and the rich crimson, sweetly scented flowers are a good shape. Up to six years ago there was a plant of 'Hugh Dickson' growing on the wall of a house in Yorkshire which to my knowledge was forty years old, still treasured for its beauty and long-flowering season. It should be pruned in winter, taking out weak and worn-out growth; long, young growth is then tipped back to ripe wood.

Hybrid Musks are a mixture of so many breeding lines, Multiflora, Noisette, and Hybrid tea, which have produced a race of recurrent-flowering, strong-growing shrubs. Pruning consists of removing dead flower trusses, and then removing weak, diseased, or worn-out shoots in winter to encourage young shoots. I once designed a double border planted with shrub

Above: Climbing rose 'American Pillar' framing the lovely avenues of La Roseraie de l'Haÿ les Roses

Right: *Rosa* 'Hugh Dickson'
Far right: *Rosa rugosa* 'Rubra'

roses, including Hybrid Musks, which in June was such an interplay of muted colour tones and fragrance that years later I still remember it with intense pleasure.

'Buff Beauty', with well-formed blooms of apricot-yellow, was well represented because cuttings rooted so easily. 'Cornelia' flowered continuously from mid-June onwards, a deep bronze-apricot in bud, opening to buff-pink. 'Moonlight', a *R. moschata* hybrid with the other parent unknown, is another 'Musk rose' of merit. The huge flower trusses, carried on young shoots which follow the first flush of bloom, are typically musk-scented.

The species *R. rugosa* is a native of northern China, Korea, and Japan, where it grows wild in sandy soils near the coast. Yet in complete contradiction to what I could have expected, both budded stock and plants grown from cuttings grew well in a Yorkshire garden where the soil is a heavy clay. Though *R. rugosa* has been cultivated for centuries in China, it did not make a positive influence on European gardens until the late nineteenth century. Breeders then appeared to note the hardiness, disease resistance and flower colour. *R. rugosa* cross-pollinates so readily with other roses that it is not surprising there are so many varieties of this shrub on offer. All old, spent stems and twig-like, non-productive growth should be removed during winter.

Within the *R. rugosa* species, the form 'Rubra' is a magnificent shrub where space can be afforded, the deep crimson flowers relieved by cream-coloured stamens. In autumn the leaves colour pale yellow and show the dark red hips to advantage. Also showing definite *rugosa* characteristics, 'Roseraie de l'Hay' has what could be described as a luxuriously coloured, velvet-textured flower. The crimson-purple petals are delightful seen with sunlight shining through them. The plant is lovely in association with Regal lilies, whose white flowers contrast with the regal purple-crimson of the rose. Of so many so-called *'rugosa'* hybrids it can be said that the relationship is hard to identify, but not so with 'Sarah Van Fleet', which in dark green foliage and upright growth mirrors its ancestry. The freely produced flowers are pink, semi-double, and sweetly scented.

Breeding continues, and each year new Hybrid shrub roses are released on to the market. Most have the perpetual flowering habit, but in many cases they lack that impossible-to-define specific called 'character'. 'Fritz Nobis' with *R. rubiginosa* as the seed parent is, amongst the newcomers, good value. The HT-shaped flowers are pink with darker shading, and the lovely clove scent is retained. 'Nevada' is said to have the excellent *R. moyesii* as one parent. A large bush, its branches 7 feet (2 m) long arch over to display a mass of creamy-white flowers, each measuring 4 to 5 inches (10 to 13 cm) across, making a garden pageant of extravagant beauty. As with nearly all roses, both species and hybrids, semi-hard or hardwood cuttings root very easily.

That most excellent rose 'Queen Elizabeth' is too tall for inclusion with the Floribunda bedding roses. Growing to a height of 6 feet (1·8 m), it gives the best display when grown as a hedge or grouped in a shrub border. Silver-pink, HT-shaped flowers open in clusters for four or five months from late June.

Climbing and Rambling roses contribute so much to the beauty of gardens, covering house walls, fences, and unsightly buildings with a living screen of magnificent flowers. There are so many to choose from in the various groups: strong-growing 'Kiftsgate' and 'Wedding Day', which are too large for any but the very big garden, to the ramblers like 'Violette', with clusters of flowers of such a dark purple that they would be lost shadows were it not for the contrasting yellow stamens.

R. sempervirens, *R. wichuriana*, and *R. multiflora* all contribute blood or bone to their virtue. I can only select those which have served me well. For the sixty-two years since being introduced 'Albertine' has carved a special niche in gardeners'

Rosa 'Kew Rambler'

Above: *Rosa* 'Nevada'
Right: *Rosa* 'New Dawn'

affections. Though there is only one display of flowers, in midsummer, the dark green leaves vanish under a mound of multi-toned salmon on pink on buff flowers. Both as a Climber and as a free-growing shrub this is a rose to grow fond of; the colour and fragrance make it one of the choice *wichuriana* Ramblers.

'Félicité et Perpétue' is an old, bone-hardy Rambler to which I owe a debt of gratitude. For six years it disguised one of the ugliest buildings ever to pollute a garden. The foliage is practically perennial, the flowers are pink in bud opening to white – millions of crimp-petalled pompons. The fragrance is delicately positive without being intrusive. 'Kew Rambler' deserves to be better known, having been introduced seventy years ago, and earned an Award of Merit sixty years ago. The specimen in my charge clothed an interlap wooden screen 25 feet (7·6 m) long with masking greenery; in June the flowers were dark pink with a white eye, until, as October came, masses of small orange hips appeared. 'Mermaid', the result of a cross between *R. bracteata* and a Tea rose, is tender and best grown on a sheltered wall. There it will open a succession of single yellow blooms 4 inches (10 cm) wide from June to October. Pruning should be restricted to removing dead or damaged branches.

'New Dawn' is one of those roses that are guaranteed to grow and flower anywhere and to please, if not to earn unqualified adoration. It is a good rose for general planting, and has silver-pink, scented flowers perpetually during the summer. No one who has seen the Rambler 'Wedding Day' growing into the apple tree then trailing over the path in the East Lambrooke Manor garden in June – a white-petalled, orange-scented curtain – will forget this exquisite picture. It is vigorous indeed, but a Rambler which can be left very much to its own devices once established.

The so-called 'Old-fashioned' roses would not have survived in competition with so many modern introductions if they were not such interesting and lovely plants. Old roses are more perennial in character than the HT and Floribunda bedding-rose varieties, important though these two groups may be.

9
Modern Roses
(Hybrid tea and Floribunda)

The modern bedding rose is entirely a product of the plant breeder's art. With one root of the family tree in China, the other in Europe, man was the marriage broker who brought the widely separate cultures together; for, while the European gardeners were busily raising new varieties from crosses between *Rosa gallica*, *R. moschata*, *R. phoenicea*, *R. damascena*, and others, so the Chinese with an even larger number of species to work with were themselves developing entirely separate groups of hybrids. All these roses, European and Chinese – or, more correctly, Western and Eastern Asian – though variable in themselves offered only a limited programme to the plant breeders. The bringing together of the separate cultures broadened the scope and possibility of variation to an almost unlimited extent. In the latter half of the eighteenth century *R. chinensis* arrived in Europe and in due course worked a transformation in the habit of growth and flowering period of our garden roses.

The modern, dwarf-growing, repeat-flowering Hybrid tea rose is infinitely more valuable as a garden decoration than the Shrub rose, which flowers only once a year. Characteristically, the flower has a definite, pointed bud. This opens to show many velvet-like petals, all of which, in a good show rose, will be reflexed and arranged perfectly to provide the central cone. Curiously, in the wild state *R. chinensis* – soon dubbed the 'China rose' – is often a climber 20 feet (6 m) high. The repeat-flowering form is a bush only 4 feet (1·2 m) high, known in Chinese gardens, according to historians, since the sixteenth century. Then early in the nineteenth century came *R. gigantea*, the Chinese rose which established the habit of continuous flowering, not just in the Hybrid tea roses but in many of the Shrub roses also, notably the Hybrid Musks and Perpetuals. Some dictionaries still list this most noteworthy rose under *R. odorata*, while the latest edition of Bean places it under *R. gigantea*. Piece by piece the essential parts of the genealogical jigsaw link together. *R. chinensis* contributed the repeat-flowering character, while *R. gigantea* added the high, pointed shape and characteristic scent to the individual blooms. In European gardens *R. gigantea* proved tender, flourishing outdoors only in the milder parts of the country, a quality inherent in its tea-rose

A colourful bed of Floribunda roses at Parc de la Tête d'Or, Lyons

progeny. But from China came the famous ancestral roses, popularly known as the 'stud' roses: 'Parson's Pink, 'Hume's Blush Tea-Scented China', and others, including 'Slater's Crimson', which is thought to be the parent of the 'Portland Rose'. To simplify a rather complex genealogical tree a cross between one of the Damask roses with a hybrid China rose resulted in the Hybrid Perpetuals, which, from 1825, held a proud place in gardens. Unlike the tea roses, Hybrid Perpetuals are quite hardy and need no protection, whether grown as dwarf bush or climber. Hundreds of varieties were raised, but the first Hybrid Perpetual is generally agreed to have been 'Rose du Roi'.

In 1870 there occurred another one of those happy accidents which mark significant milestones in rose history. In a nursery near Lyon, amongst a batch of seedling *R. multiflora* roses of Japanese origin, a M. Guillot noticed a white form, which he called 'Paquerette'. The accidental pollen exchange was thought to have been between multiflora and dwarf pink China or Fairy Rose. Seed harvested from the white-flowered 'Paquerette' grew on to give two dwarf seedlings with pompon flower heads, the first Polyantha. From such a modest, inauspicious beginning came an entirely new race of roses to compete with the HT for pride of place in our gardens. It is even more extraordinary that out of this second generation only two of the seedlings were shrubs and continuous-flowering; the remainder were once-flowering dwarf climbers. No doubt, the crosses between the Polypon or Polyantha and HT which produced 'Cecile Brunner' were made soon after. Even a hundred years after this is a most desirable, perfectly formed pale-pink, shaded-yellow Miniature rose. 'Perle d'Or', even more exquisite, appeared four years later. Dwarf in habit, the perfectly shaped buds open pale orange-pink and are very fragrant.

Notable though these two early hybrid Polyantha roses may be, it was a rose breeder in Denmark who took the rose world by assault when in 1924 he introduced a distinct group of roses. The Poulsen roses (as they came to be called) were achieved by crossing Polypon (Polyantha) into Hybrid tea. Svend Poulsen took pollen from the HT 'Red Star' to fertilise the Polypom 'Orleans'. From this union two seedlings emerged, one, with semi-double, medium-sized bright rose-pink flowers on strong upstanding stems, was duly named 'Else Poulsen'. The other, though equally vigorous, had bright, cherry-red single flowers and was called 'Kirsten Poulsen'. The garden in which I worked as a youth had a hedge of 'Kirsten Poulsen' to divide the rose garden. The strong, upright growth is ideally suited to the purpose. Other Poulsen varieties followed, 'Karen Poulsen' and 'Poulsen's Pink' being the best known. The name that was

A lovely combination of Floribunda roses and a Standard rose in a public park

Above and right: *Rosa* 'The Fairy'

originally given to the new race of roses, Hybrid Polyantha, has subsequently been changed to 'Floribunda'. These do not possess the size of individual blooms when compared to their rival, the Hybrid Tea rose. Here the flowers are less pointed in shape and are borne in large trusses continually throughout the rose season.

Of all the bedding roses, HT, Polyantha (or Floribunda), no single variety has achieved greater popularity than 'Peace'. Raised by F. Meilland in France, the breeding line includes some illustrious roses, 'George Dickson' and 'Margaret McGredy' being two well known in this country. The seedling 'Peace' flowered in 1935, stocks were budded in 1936 and blossomed the same autumn. What must have been the feeling of M. Meilland on seeing the first flower fully open! Large, full-bodied, each yellow petal edged with pink, and the shape exceptional. Add to these the qualities of vigorous constitution, glossy, disease-resistant foliage, and virtually weather-proof flowers. What a proud justification for a lifetime's work! In my experience 'Peace' should be only lightly pruned or growth is made at the expense of flowers.

Climbing 'sports' of HT roses do occur; even the re-doubtable 'Peace' has a climbing offspring which, unfortunately, is shy of flower. Why some HT produce climbing branches is, no doubt, explained by the presence of a Climber rose, *R. chinensis*,

Floribundas
Left: *Rosa* 'Mountbatten'
Top: *Rosa* 'Iceberg'
Above: *Rosa* 'Evelyn Fison'

Floribundas
Top: *Rosa* 'Anne Cocker'
Above: *Rosa* 'Anne Harkness'
Right: *Rosa* 'Picasso'

in their ancestry. Occasionally the mutation which brought forth a dwarf repeat-flowering shrub reverts to type, and we get a climbing HT – which proves yet again what a splendidly accommodating plant the rose is!

In the majority of cases roses are propagated by budding. This consists of taking a plump, dormant bud from a healthy shoot, and then grafting it on to suitable root-stock, usually in July and August. Root-stocks can be bought by an amateur grower who is keen to raise new roses for home use. The stocks used are *canina* or selections from it, *laxa, multiflora*, and, for standard roses, *rugosa* is still popular. The stocks, which preferably should be the thickness of the little finger or a drawing pencil, are lined out 4 to 6 inches (10 to 15 cm) apart the previous autumn or winter.

Take the buds from the middle of a healthy branch which has just flowered. Cut the whole branch and strip off the leaves, except for an inch of stalk under each bud, which is left as a handle. The thorns are also removed. Holding the branch firmly, take a sharp budding knife, make a cut half an inch (1·2 cm) below the selected bud. Then, half an inch above the bud insert the knife at a right angle to the stem and draw it down under the first cut. The piece of bark with bud attached can be lifted clear. Always handle it by the leaf stalk, for on no account must the piece of bark known as the shield be allowed to get dirty.

Clean the soil away from the base of the selected stock; wipe it if necessary with a soft cloth. Make a horizontal cut at the neck of the stock, then a vertical cut from near the root up to meet it. The two cuts form a letter T. Gently lift the edges of the bark, insert the shield and fix it firmly in place with raffia, rubber, or plastic ties.

Roses can, of course, be grown from seed, but only species will breed true; hybrid seed will produce a rare old mixture – most of them useless.

Most roses can be propagated from cuttings taken in September to October from well-ripened shoots of the current year's growth. Cuttings should be about 8 inches (20 cm) long or more – up to 15 inches (38 cm) in some cases. Remove all the leaves from the bottom third of the cutting, then after dipping the base in rooting powder dibble them into a sandy compost soil or cutting mixture made up of 2 parts soil, 2 parts sharp sand, 1 part peat. The following autumn all cuttings which have rooted can be transplanted to flowering quarters.

Propagation by layering is the method used to increase stocks of Rambler roses, particularly the *wichuriana* hybrids. Indeed, this is the easiest way, for quite often shoots which touch the soil will root naturally with no help from the gardener. Select a shoot of the previous year's growth, twist or wound a section which can be conveniently pegged down to the ground to stimulate rooting, then bury the treated section in a sandy compost. A heavy stone or peg is essential to hold the layer firmly in place. The following

Right (all Hybrid Tea):
Rosa 'Peace'
Rosa 'Pink Favourite'
Rosa 'Whisky Mac'
Rosa 'Alec's Red'

Far right:
Floribunda roses make a good foil for yucca in full flower at Parc de la Tête d'Or, Lyons

Rosa 'Silver Jubilee' (Hybrid Tea)

autumn the layers will be rooted well enough for lifting. This method is not suitable for climbing HT or Floribunda roses, which are better budded on vigorous root-stock.

Roses are cursed with the reputation that they will grow anywhere. This quite often means they are rammed in with no thought given to their cultural requirements. That they grow and flower is a tribute to their resilience, though compared with roses grown in well-prepared soil and properly cared for they are mere shadows of their real selves. Roses should be planted in full sun, away from trees, whose roots compete with them for nutriment. There is also less risk of disease if the site is open with free air circulation.

Shrub roses make admirable feature plants in the ornamental border. Bedding roses, the HT, and Floribunda look very attractive against the green background of a lawn.

Roses thrive in a heavy soil so long as it is well drained and cultivated. However, all soils whatever their composition, will grow roses if plenty of farm manure, compost, or similar material is worked in two or three months before the date set for planting. The finest roses I ever grew were planted in what were previously grass fields, which gives some indication of the soil condition they enjoy.

Arguments about whether autumn or spring planting is best are never resolved. After growing many thousand roses, autumn is the time I choose, providing the soil is in good condition. Quite often the nurseries lift the bushes early in the autumn, so they

might as well be in my care as in theirs. Also the rose sends out
new roots in midwinter – late January to February – so they
establish much more quickly than if the planting were delayed
until spring. Any bushes planted later than March should be
puddled in – have their roots dipped in what is virtually liquid
mud as a precaution against their drying out. Before planting,
whatever the season, I shorten back the roots with a pair of
secateurs or a sharp knife. This stimulates the growth of fine
feeding roots.

Dig a hole large and deep enough to accommodate the roots
comfortably, spread the fibres out horizontally, then work in
about 4 inches (10 cm) of soil amongst the roots. Firm this down
with your feet, then complete the filling in with soil from the bed.
The junction between the root and stem (budding point) should
then be about 1 inch (2·5 cm) below the soil surface.

I prefer to prune established roses in early March. First cut

An attractive corner
at the Bagatelle, Paris

away all dead, weak, or damaged branches, then prune all the really strong branches back to about six buds, the rest back to three buds. There can be no set rules: the severity or otherwise of pruning depends very much on the variety. Hard pruning of a strong-growing variety like 'Peace' brings more wood and no flowers. Floribunda–Polyantha are not pruned quite so hard. Again, I first clean out all moribund or unwanted branches, then cut back the remainder to seven or eight buds.

Climbing roses should be pruned in their formative years to build up a permanent framework of branches. Short growths which spring from framework branches I cut back to three buds. Strong young shoots are trained in to replace any of the original framework as required.

To get a continuous display of flowers from June to autumn, all roses need to be fed: 2 oz (57 g) of balanced fertiliser to the square yard (0·8 m) in mid-April, plus a mulch of rotted manure, peat, compost or whatever is available in early May. Then in early July a further 2 oz (57 g) of fertiliser per square yard will keep the roses in flower. They also require a constant supply of moisture throughout the growing season. A mulch of organic matter put on the soil will help, but during dry weather watering with either a sprinkler or hosepipe so as to thoroughly saturate the soil will be of great benefit to the plants.

Suckers are shoots which grow from the root-stock and should be removed. Carefully trace the sucker shoot to its point of origin and then pull, NOT cut it away. Suckers are a result of incorrect planting or digging amongst established roses which has damaged the roots.

Pests and disease will attack even the well-maintained rose garden. There are on the market five or six products available to combat any disease or pest which has the temerity to attack our roses. Most important, correctly identify the pest or disease; then take steps to control it. Fungicides and pesticides used on the 'blanket' principle to control every scourge that could infest the garden can be dangerous. It is far better to know the culprit, and use a chemical which deals specifically with it – obeying the manufacturer's instructions exactly.

In a rose garden where the plants are pruned, fed, and watered correctly, I have always found two or three sprays to be enough. A three-tier programme would be a systemic insecticide in mid-May to control the first aphis (green-fly) infestation; in mid- to late-June a combined systemic insecticide and fungicide (green-fly and mildew control); in later August it may be necessary to repeat the fungal spray.

Fortunately, roses are the easiest of plants to grow, providing there is no lack of that most excellent fertiliser, common sense. Over the hundreds of years that they have been grown and admired they have earned a unique place in garden history and legend. The story has not yet been fully unfolded, and there are still species which have not been used by the hybridiser. Who knows what colours may evolve next year, perhaps a rose the colour of a Gentian or Delphinium? With roses no dream is impossible.

Below: *Rosa* 'Just Joey' (Hybrid Tea)

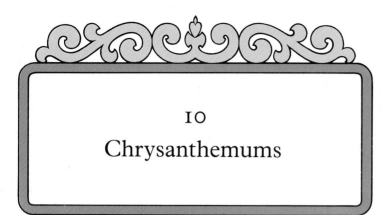

10
Chrysanthemums

Chrysos, 'golden' *anthos*, 'flower' – such is its meaning, though the word 'chrysanthemum' conjures up a picture in the mind's eye of mist-shrouded autumn days. The flower, by comparison with long-established favourites like the rose, is a newcomer. In 1789 a M. Blancard introduced three chrysanthemums from the Far East into Marseilles. Only one, 'Old Purple', survived, and stock eventually found its way to England. The story of the chrysanthemum in England began in 1796 with the 327th plate of the *Botanical Magazine*, which showed a plant which grew in Mr Colville's Nursery in King's Road, Chelsea. Between 1820 and 1830 upwards of forty varieties, either by means of seed or plants, were imported, and the foundations were laid of what is now a considerable industry. Once the hybridisers had succeeded in setting and ripening seed on plants grown in this country, the production of new varieties could begin in earnest.

The so-called 'Autumn' chrysanthemums are descendants of the white-flowered Chinese *Chrysanthemum morifolium (sinensis)*, or yellow-flowered *C. indicum* species. In 1846 Robert Fortune, a plant hunter and explorer extraordinary, sent home to England roots of the Chusan daisy, which was to be the parent of a whole new race, the very popular Pompon varieties.

Though of the same family as the daisy which stars so many of our lawns with white, it is only in the wild species that the chrysanthemum shows a marked resemblance to our modest British weed. Both *C. morifolium (sinensis)* and *C. indicum* show a yellow disc surrounded by ray florets. By selection the fertile central disc florets have been replaced by the more brightly coloured female ray petals. Double flowers are more sought after for garden decoration and floristry than the wild singles. Indeed, it is uncommon, for obvious reasons, to find full double forms of any plants in the wild, for if the bisexual disc florets have become unisexual female florets, the plant cannot set seed to reproduce itself. Full doubles are only preserved in our gardens by vegetative propagation. They are a product of the hybridiser's art, and are perpetuated by the gardener's skill. Even when giving the appearance of being full double, quite often the chrysanthemum preserves sufficient of the disc florets to produce seed which is of value in hybridisation.

Chrysanthemum rubellum 'Bonny Blush'

Much of the work of hybridising had already been done before the flower reached Europe. Since then, the process of selection and improvement on an established foundation has continued to give an ever-increasing range of hybrids, collectively known as *Chrysanthemum × hortorum*.

Before dealing with the intricacies of the classification of *C. × hortorum* and its cultivation under garden conditions, it will be helpful to describe the other species which, though not so widely grown, are useful garden plants. Four chrysanthemums are

native to this country: Corn marigold, *C. segetum*; Ox-eye daisy, *C. leucanthemum*; Feverfew, *C. parthenium*; and the debatable *C. vulgare*, the Common tansy, which is more often listed as *Tanacetum*. All flower in the summer time. Feverfew, which is often in abundance in or around gardens, is recommended in herbals as a treatment for migraine. Certainly, anyone who can relish the strong-tasting leaves deserves to be cured. Migraine sufferers have assured me it is effective.

In all there are over a hundred species widely distributed throughout the world. *C. alpinum*, a good garden plant, is easily raised from seed. The annual species are colourful plants and are usually sown direct into the open where they are to flower. Most of the perennial species are well suited by conditions in the herbaceous or mixed border, providing that the soil is well drained. Some species are valuable as a source of pyrethrum powder, a well-known insecticide still used in gardens, particularly as a control for white-fly.

C. carinatum is usually listed in seed catalogues as *C. tricolor* in the section devoted to hardy annuals. They are excellent value, whether grown for cut flowers or garden display. Seeds are sown in well-prepared soil in late April into shallow drills 12 inches (30 cm) apart, then thinned out after germination to a final spacing of 18 inches (46 cm) apart in the rows. The varieties on offer are often banded or zoned in contrasting colours. Stronger-growing *C. × spectabile* varieties, which are much in demand as cut flowers, grow up to 36 inches (91 cm) in height, and so need more space.

C. cinerariifolium is the source of pyrethrum insecticides, and is not widely grown in gardens. *C. coccineum*, parent of the extremely popular pyrethrum, was introduced from the Caucasus in 1807. Most of the varieties will thrive if given an open, fertile soil, fully exposed to all the available sunshine. Contrary to my experience with many herbaceous perennials, pyrethrums are

Above left: *Chrysanthemum alpinum*
Above: *Chrysanthemum segetum*

best lifted and divided in late July, though early spring will do as second best. There are some delightful colour forms available, some double or semi-double, though I much prefer single-flowered sorts. The safest plan when selecting varieties is to visit a nursery offering stock and see the plants in flower, so avoiding disappointment. One word of warning: I never succeeded in growing pyrethrum in a heavy clay soil; the best results always came from those plants accommodated in medium to light loam.

A most reliable annual species can be found in *C. coronarium* from the Mediterranean region. It is about 3 to 4 feet (0·9 to 1·9 m) high with wide-branching stems bearing pale green leaves and cream or yellow flowers. The *C. nanum compactum* and *C. spatiosum* are selected forms of neater growth and more varied colours. They are very useful for direct sowing to fill gaps in the shrub or herbaceous border, and will continue in flower right through into the autumn.

As would be expected of a plant from the Canary Islands, Marguerite or Paris daisy, *C. frutescens*, is not reliably hardy. Overwintered in a frost-free greenhouse, then planted out with the summer bedding, it remains in bloom throughout the summer. A shrubby, dome-shaped bush 3 feet (0·9 m) high, covered in yellow-centred daisy flowers appeals to most tastes when surrounded by blue- or red-flowered bedding plants. The Paris daisy is available in shades of white, pink, or yellow, also with a choice of double flowers.

There are few more robust perennials than the Shasta daisy, *C. maximum*. The large white flowers of 'Esther Read', 'Wirral Supreme', and 'Bishopstone' have featured in borders down my

Chrysanthemum maximum

Chrysanthemum parthenium

gardening years. They are most effective in herbaceous borders along with other popular perennials or (my preference) planted amongst Shrub roses where they act as a foil to the red-purple of 'Gypsy Boy', or 'Chiante'. Though happy in light soils, the strongest plants I looked after were rooted in a strong-bodied but well-drained clay. Division offers a ready means of increase when new stock is needed.

Though possessed of medical virtue Feverfew, *C. parthenium*, is best known as a dwarf edging to summer bedding. As with many native plants, 'Feverfew' takes so kindly to cultivation that it can become a nuisance. Confusingly, in seed catalogues this species is often listed under *Matricaria exima*. Seed sown in late March will give well-grown plants for bedding out in late May. 'Golden Ball' and 'Snow Puff' will make good foils to the more violently aggressive bedding plants. The rounded hummocks of strongly scented leaves, which seldom grow more

Chrysanthemum 'Imp'
(Hardy Perennial)

Top and above:
Chrysanthemum 'Bunty' at
Bressingham Gardens, Norfolk

than 12 inches (30 cm) high are covered throughout the summer in full double button, mini chrysanthemum flowers. Legend has it that early botanists named the species *C. parthenium* because it saved the life of a workman who became giddy and fell from one of the walls while building the Parthenon. Such thoughts are the very romance of gardening.

Certainly, *C. uliginosum* is the most vigorously invasive of all the family that I have grown. Root-like underground stems push out from the parent to colonise new land far in excess of any space the beauty of the flowers deserves. Stalks 4 feet (1·2 m) high display sprays of white Dog daisy flowers in September.

Undoubtedly, it is the hybrid *C. × hortorum* which has made the biggest impact on the private garden and the horticultural industry. Reflecting on the origins of the extravagantly shaped, highly coloured varieties which grace gardens and greenhouses today, I could not help wondering what the thoughts of the man who made that first cross between *C. morifolium* (*sinensis*) and *C. indicum* were. Did he, three thousand years ago, understand the reasons for cross-pollination and carry out the operation as a deliberate attempt to produce a new race of plants, or was it an insect-aided accident? I doubt if any other single act of hybridisation in plants will ever equal that of the unknown Chinese gardener before gardens existed in Europe. What is certain is that chrysanthemums were grown in large quantities throughout China and Japan five hundred years before the birth of Christ.

Beginning with the Chinese hybrids with incurved florets, continuing on to the reflexing, shaggy-flowered Japanese types, mix in the Pompon-flowered Chusan chrysanthemum, let them all cross-hybridise, and the result is a modern florist's chrysanthemum in an almost infinite variety of shapes and almost every colour except blue. Specialist societies are not only an inevitable result, they become an absolute essential to bring order out of the chaos caused by a proliferation of new varieties.

The method of classification is based on the shape of the bloom, whether single or double, on how the florets are developed, and their shape and distribution on the central disc. Unfortunately, the majority of the varieties on offer, especially the large-flowered forms, do not make trouble-free hardy perennials. From the cutting stage to flowering they need a routine of staking, disbudding, and feeding which few other of our garden flowers demand. The end product is full justification for all the devoted care, a specialist would argue – a flower whose colour and shape epitomise the summit of perfection.

There are hardy or nearly hardy varieties, some which would be termed old-fashioned by a specialist grower. All will do well in fertile, free-draining soil, producing a crop of flowers which brighten the autumn borders without making any more demands on our time than any other quality herbaceous perennial. For years I grew a yellow-flowered, bone-hardy *C.* 'Jante Welles', one of the most delightful plants to grace the autumn. Unfortunately, I lost stock when changing gardens and have never been able to replace it. Such plants are well worth searching for. *C. rubellum* 'Clara Curtis' is one of a number of good border varieties which are still available.

The Korean hybrids will survive with no more protection than a cold frame in winter. They are produced by crossing *C. coreanum* with a pink-flowered Pompon variety, and are delightfully compact perennials of 18 to 24 inches (46 to 61 cm), producing a profusion of flower sprays into late autumn. I grew the Otley Koreans for years, treating them like any other hardy perennial, lifting and dividing the roots as necessary, and found them excellent. The modern Koreans are less robustly hardy and need lifting indoors for the winter. Classification of the florists' varieties of chrysanthemum is usually under six, possibly now

Good border varieties
Above left:
Chrysanthemum rubellum
'Pennine Signal'
Centre:
Chrysanthemum rubellum
'Clara Curtis'
Above right:
Chrysanthemum rubellum
'Buttercup'

Right:
Chrysanthemum 'Otley Beauty'
(Korean hybrid)

Top left (Incurved):
Chrysanthemum 'Peter Doig'
Top centre (Reflexed):
Chrysanthemum 'Joyce Stevenson'
Top right (Single-flowered):
Chrysanthemum 'Pennine Serene'
Left (Intermediate):
Chrysanthemum 'Bill Wade'

Below (Pompon):
Chrysanthemum 'Rosebud'
Below right (Double-flowered):
Chrysanthemum 'Amber Margaret'

seven headings, although for show purposes these primary groups are divided into sections and sub-sections *ad infinitum*.

The seven main groups are as follows:
1 *Incurved* – where the florets curve inwards to make a perfect globe;
2 *Reflexed* – where the outer florets particularly curve upwards, partially or completely;
3 *Intermediate* – where the florets incurve loosely or irregularly;
4 *Anemone-flowered* – single but with a raised central cushion;
5 *Pompon* – small-flowered as the name implies, developed from the Chusan chrysanthemum.
6 *Singles* – varieties with no more than five rows of ray florets around a daisy centre;
7 *Miscellaneous* – this group contains a very mixed bag.

Though I have grown chrysanthemums for years, the attempts at detailed classification still confuse me.

All types of chrysanthemum are best propagated by means of cuttings. The time varies according to type. Roots are lifted from selected varieties once the flowers have faded, then stored in a frost-free place. These are started into growth, usually by spraying them overhead with water as cuttings are required. The young shoots which make the best cuttings are short-jointed, 2 to 3 inches (5 to 8 cm) long. Those which come from below the soil are to be preferred to shoots which grow out of the old stem. They can be rooted in a sandy compost over bottom heat in seven to ten days, and potted off into John Innes or peat-based compost for growing on. After suitable acclimatisation, the plants are moved outdoors in late May for the summer.

If left to grow unhindered a chrysanthemum plant will continue until an embryo bud appears at the stem tip; this is called a 'natural break bud'. It usually shrivels, and side shoots develop from leaf axils down the stem to produce a number of flower buds.

By stopping the young plants when they are 6 inches (15 cm) high, and not allowing them to grow up to the natural break bud stage, the side shoots develop from the axils much earlier. By restricting the number of side shoots and thinning the flower buds down to one per stem, the resulting blooms are much larger and of better form than if all buds were permitted to open. With some varieties, better-quality flowers are produced by stopping not only the main stem, but also the side shoots (first crown) allowing a second lot of shoots to break; this is called 'second crown flowering'. The time it takes for a plant to produce buds after the first stop is about eight weeks: if the stop is made in May, flowers will bloom in late July or August. The second stop provides a further seven- or eight-week delay; the plants so treated will flower in a heated greenhouse in November to December.

One important point to note is that the flower buds which form at the various stages (that is, natural breaks, first or second crown), develop into very different flowers depending on the number of ray florets produced. Usually when buying new plants from a nurseryman a list of instructions is supplied for each variety – whether to flower on natural break, first or second crown. This is not something it is nice to know, but MUST be known if top-quality blooms are the aim.

Development of the chrysanthemum flower bud is also influenced by day length. Only when subject to a certain number of hours of darkness do the buds develop – the chrysanthemum is what is termed a 'short-day plant', flowering in autumn. It can be persuaded to flower in spring or summer by keeping it under black polythene covers for a set number of hours. Cuttings treated with a chemical which restricts the distance between leaf joints in order to keep the plants dwarf, and then subjected to the dark treatment make excellent pot plants for home decoration – just another facet of the commercial exploitation of a very popular flower.

Index